# CRIMINAL
## INVESTIGATIONS

## GANGS AND
## GANG CRIME

# CRIMINAL INVESTIGATIONS

Bank Robbery

Celebrities and Crime

Child Abduction and Kidnapping

Cons and Frauds

Crime Scene Investigation

Cybercrime

Drug Crime

Gangs and Gang Crime

Homicide

Organized Crime

Serial Killers

Terrorism

Unsolved Crimes

White-Collar Crime

# CRIMINAL
## INVESTIGATIONS

## GANGS AND GANG CRIME

# MICHAEL NEWTON

CONSULTING EDITOR: **JOHN L. FRENCH**,

CRIME SCENE SUPERVISOR,
BALTIMORE POLICE CRIME LABORATORY

**CHELSEA HOUSE** PUBLISHERS

An imprint of Infobase Publishing

**CRIMINAL INVESTIGATIONS: Gangs and Gang Crime**

Copyright © 2008 by Infobase Publishing

Chelsea House
An imprint of Infobase Publishing
132 West 31st Street
New York NY 10001

**Library of Congress Cataloging-in-Publication Data**
Newton, Michael, 1951-
Gangs and gang crime / Michael Newton. — 1st ed.
p. cm. — (Criminal investigations)
Includes bibliographical references and index.
P  ISBN-13: 978-0-7910-9408-2 (alk. paper)
ISBN-10: 0-7910-9408-1 (alk. paper)
1.  Gangs—United States—Juvenile literature. 2.  Gangs—United
States—Case studies—Juvenile literature. 3.  Violent crimes—United
States—Juvenile literature. 4.  Juvenile delinquency—United States—
Juvenile literature.  I. Title. II. Series.
HV6439.U5N49 2008                364.1'0660973—dc22
2008007557

Text design by Erika K. Arroyo
Cover design by Ben Peterson

*Cover:* Special agents working for Immigration and Customs Enforcement
(ICE) escort members of a Mexican gang to court following their arrests
on May 11, 2005, in New York City.

Printed in the United States of America

Bang EJB 10 9 8 7 6 5 4 3 2 1

This book is printed on acid-free paper.

# Contents

Foreword     7

Introduction     11

**1** Cracks in the Melting Pot     15

**2** Supply and Demand     23

**3** Public Enemies and Holdup Gangs     35

**4** Hell on Wheels     47

**5** Prison Gangs     55

**6** Crips and Bloods     65

**7** New World Disorder     73

**8** Gangs in Fiction and Film     83

**9** Coping with Gangs     91

Chronology     103

Endnotes     106

Bibliography     107

Further Resources     108

Index     109

About the Author     119

About the Consulting Editor     120

# Foreword

In 2000 there were 15,000 murders in the United States. During that same year about a half million people were assaulted, 1.1 million cars were stolen, 400,000 robberies took place, and more than 2 million homes and businesses were broken into. All told, in the last year of the twentieth century, there were more than 11 million crimes committed in this country.*

In 2000 the population of the United States was approximately 280 million people. If each of the above crimes happened to a separate person, only 4 percent of the country would have been directly affected. Yet everyone is in some way affected by crime. Taxes pay patrolmen, detectives, and scientists to investigate it, lawyers and judges to prosecute it, and correctional officers to watch over those convicted of committing it. Crimes against businesses cause prices to rise as their owners pass on the cost of theft and security measures installed to prevent future losses. Tourism in cities, and the money it brings in, may rise and fall in part due to stories about crime in their streets. And every time someone is shot, stabbed, beaten, or assaulted, or when someone is jailed for having committed such a crime, not only they suffer but so may their friends, family, and loved ones. Crime affects everyone.

It is the job of the police to investigate crime with the purpose of putting the bad guys in jail and keeping them there, hoping thereby to punish past crimes and discourage new ones. To accomplish this a police officer has to be many things: dedicated, brave, smart, honest, and imaginative. Luck helps, but it's not required. And there's one more virtue that should be associated with law enforcement. A good police officer is patient.

Patience is a virtue in crime fighting because police officers and detectives know something that most criminals don't. It's not a secret, but most lawbreakers don't learn it until it is too late. Criminals who make money robbing people, breaking into houses, or stealing cars; who live by dealing drugs or committing murder; who spend their days on the wrong side of the law, or commit any other crimes, must remember this: a criminal has to get away with every crime he or she commits. However, to get criminals off the street and put them behind bars, the police only have to catch a criminal once.

The methods by which police catch criminals are varied. Some are as old as recorded history and others are so new that they have yet to be tested in court. One of the first stories in the Bible is of murder, when Cain killed his brother Abel (Genesis 4:1–16). With few suspects to consider and an omniscient detective, this was an easy crime to solve. However, much later in that same work, a young man named Daniel steps in when a woman is accused of an immoral act by two elders (Daniel 13:1–63). By using the standard police practice of separating the witnesses before questioning them, he is able to arrive at the truth of the matter.

From the time of the Bible to almost present day, police investigations did not progress much further than questioning witnesses and searching the crime scene for obvious clues as to a criminal's identity. It was not until the late 1800s that science began to be employed. In 1879 the French began to use physical measurements and later photography to identify repeat offenders. In the same year a Scottish missionary in Japan used a handprint found on a wall to exonerate a man accused of theft. In 1892 a bloody fingerprint led Argentine police to charge and convict a mother of killing her children, and by 1905 Scotland Yard had convicted several criminals thanks to this new science.

Progress continued. By the 1920s scientists were using blood analysis to determine if recovered stains were from the victim or suspect, and the new field of firearms examination helped link bullets to the guns that fired them.

Nowadays, things are even harder on criminals, when by leaving behind a speck of blood, dropping a sweat-stained hat, or even taking a sip from a can of soda, they can give the police everything they need to identify and arrest them.

In the first decade of the twenty-first century the main tools used by the police include

- questioning witnesses and suspects
- searching the crime scene for physical evidence
- employing informants and undercover agents
- investigating the whereabouts of previous offenders when a crime they've been known to commit has occurred
- using computer databases to match evidence found on one crime scene to that found on others or to previously arrested suspects
- sharing information with other law enforcement agencies via the Internet
- using modern communications to keep the public informed and enlist their aid in ongoing investigations

But just as they have many different tools with which to solve crime, so too do they have many different kinds of crime and criminals to investigate. There is murder, kidnapping, and bank robbery. There are financial crimes committed by con men who gain their victim's trust or computer experts who hack into computers. There are criminals who have formed themselves into gangs and those who are organized into national syndicates. And there are those who would kill as many people as possible, either for the thrill of taking a human life or in the horribly misguided belief that it will advance their cause.

The Criminal Investigations series looks at all of the above and more. Each book in the series takes one type of crime and gives the reader an overview of the history of the crime, the methods and motives behind it, the people who have committed it, and the means by which these people are caught and punished. In this series celebrity crimes will be discussed and exposed. Mysteries that have yet to be solved will be presented. Readers will discover the truth about murderers, serial killers, and bank robbers whose stories have become myths and legends. These books will explain how criminals can separate a person from his hard-earned cash, how they prey on the weak and helpless, what is being done to stop them, and what one can do to help prevent becoming a victim.

John L. French,
Crime Scene Supervisor,
Baltimore Police Crime Laboratory

* Federal Bureau of Investigation. "Uniform Crime Reports, Crime in the United States 2000." Available online. URL: http://www.fbi.gov/ucr/00cius.htm. Accessed January 11, 2008.

# Introduction

Every major American city today is infested with gangs whose members engage in criminal activities including murder, robbery, carjacking, and drug trafficking. Some cities, like Los Angeles, number their yearly gang-related killings in the hundreds. Gangs that once fought for local "turf" with fists, knives, and baseball bats now operate on a national or international scale, earning millions of dollars each year, defending their empires with sophisticated military weapons. Many of their victims are innocent persons, gunned down in reckless drive-by shootings.

Today's mega-gangs had humble beginnings. In Colonial America (1620–1776), orphans in cities such as Boston, New York, and Philadelphia banded together for survival, begging and stealing to feed themselves and fighting rival gangs that threatened them. Those gangs were small and rarely lasted long in British colonies where even petty theft might be punished by hanging. Outside the cities, bands of "highwaymen" had slightly better luck at robbing travelers. Pirates created gangs-afloat, raiding at will from the Atlantic coast into the Gulf of Mexico and the Caribbean.

Later, as the United States spread "from sea to shining sea," waves of immigrants—Irish, Germans, Italians, Poles, Russians, and others—flocked to the land of opportunity, seeking new and better lives. What many found, instead, were filthy slums, low-paying jobs, and schools that failed to educate their children. Those children often ran the streets, unsupervised, and formed gangs, while older criminals recruited willing youths to serve them.

Psychologists often describe street gangs as surrogate (substitute) families, organized and adopted by young people whose home lives feature neglect, abandonment, and various kinds of abuse. The gang provides both acceptance and protection, while imposing rules of discipline that even rebellious delinquents secretly crave.

Indeed, gangs often dress the concept of a family in trappings of adventure that attract more members to their ranks. Many practice initiation rituals that may involve a test of courage in the face of danger. Those who pass receive their *colors,* meaning uniforms or emblems that identify them as a breed apart. All gangs have leaders who command their "soldiers." Many also have written bylaws spelling out approved activities and listing punishments for those who break the rules.

Unfortunately, most gangs include various criminal activities within their "family values." Whether it is *bopping* or *rumbling* (fighting) for turf, shoplifting, carjacking, dealing in contraband (illegal merchandise), or selling "protection" to neighborhood shops (extortion), gang members all too often break the law—and frequently in violent ways. A few gangs specify that new recruits cannot become full members until they commit a murder.

While civil leaders rage at gangs, politicians pass new laws against them, and police try to destroy them, many "average" Americans support gangs without meaning to. On one level, they look to gangs for entertainment, as if real-life criminals were movie characters from Hollywood. And on another level, millions of Americans take full advantage of illegal services that gangs provide.

Gangs have been entertaining newspaper subscribers in America since highwaymen like "Captain Thunderbolt" and "Captain Lightfoot" menaced pilgrims in colonial New England. Later generations followed the exploits of gang leaders ranging from New York's Monk Eastman to Missouri's Frank and Jesse James. The "Roaring Twenties" produced America's first celebrity gangsters, whose media nicknames— "Scarface," "Bugs," "Mad Dog," and so on—made them seem larger than life. Thirty years later, television brought notorious gangsters and their crimes into living rooms from coast to coast.

And America loved it.

The criminal adventures of 1920s bootleggers or 1930s bank-robbers rivaled those of any character in newspaper comic strips or Hollywood serials—and they were *real.* In the 1950s and 1960s, motorcycle gangs roared across the landscape, leaving chaos and thrills in their wake. A later generation in America's blighted inner cities lavished heroworship on ruthless drug dealers, whose crimes lifted them from poverty to riches.

At the same time, countless Americans freely participate in criminal activities controlled by gangs from major cities to the smallest rural towns. From the mid-nineteenth century to the present day, gangs have controlled various goods and services banned by law, which "honest" citizens demand, such as illegal gambling, prostitution, drugs, and a wide range of *bootleg* merchandise ranging from untaxed cigarettes and liquor to pirated films and computer software.

The cost of such items extends beyond their black-market sales price. As author Fred Cook explained in his book *A Two-Dollar Bet Means Murder* (1961), gangs are not simply involved in *victimless* crimes. The same gangsters who take "innocent" illegal bets on sporting events or sell bootleg DVDs of the latest action movie also commit crimes including murder, robbery, arson, rape, and human trafficking. They bribe and corrupt our government leaders and law enforcement officers. Despite gang members' claims that "we only kill each other," their violence often spills over to innocent victims. Some gangs—like the El Rukns of Illinois—even stand accused of plotting with foreign terrorists to massacre helpless civilians. Cook's observations thus remain true today, as proceeds from "victimless" crimes finance violent acts committed by organized criminals, terrorists, and drug users who rob to support their addiction.

*Gangs and Gang Crime* examines the history and operations of gangs in America from the nineteenth century to the present day, along with the techniques used by law enforcement and forensic scientists to solve and punish gang-related crimes. The text includes nine chapters, plus a historical chronology of American gang activity, with sources for further research into gangs, their behavior, and their crimes.

Chapter 1 examines the growth of gangs, both in eastern cities and on the western frontier, from America's early days to 1920, when a nationwide ban on liquor offered clever gangsters a fast-lane ticket to fame and fortune.

Chapter 2 reviews the era of Prohibition (1920–33), when illegal beer and whiskey sales turned petty gangsters into millionaires, and compares that period of "booze wars" to America's modern "war on drugs."

Chapter 3 follows the brief and violent careers of bank-robbing "public enemies" who mimicked Jesse James and other Wild West bandits during the Great Depression of the 1930s, prompting a rash of new laws to suppress gangsterism.

Chapter 4 traces the rise of motorcycle gangs since World War II, evolving from local cliques of unwashed hooligans and "party animals" into global networks trading in drugs, weapons, and murder.

Chapter 5 probes the murky world of American prison gangs, whose vicious power and criminal commerce often extends beyond barbed wire and brick walls into the heart of everyday society.

Chapter 6 charts the development of America's largest and most violent ghetto gangs, the Crips and Bloods, from local fighting cliques to nationwide armies of drug-dealing killers, lately transformed by the media into social icons.

Chapter 7 describes some of the newer ethnic gangs—Russian, Jamaican, Chinese, Vietnamese, and others—that have colonized America over the past quarter-century, battling each other and older, established gangs for a piece of the nationwide criminal action.

Chapter 8 compares the gangland of novels and Hollywood films to gritty street-level reality, noting the similarities and glaring differences between fact and fiction.

Chapter 9 details and evaluates law enforcement efforts to suppress illegal gangs through a variety of methods, including new laws and strict prosecution, improved education, and other forms of intervention.

Gangs are *everyone's* problem in modern America. In one way or another, their violence and other criminal activities touch each and every one of us.

# Cracks in
# the Melting Pot

*"Give me your tired, your poor, your huddled masses yearning to breathe free. . . ."*

That message, inscribed on the Statue of Liberty in 1886, invites immigrants of all nations to find homes in the United States. The United States is a nation of transplanted races, religions, and cultures, merged—at least in theory—to become one people in the "melting pot" that is America.

Sadly, the process does not always work.

Over the past four centuries, each group of new arrivals has met opposition and discrimination from the groups that came before it. Each in turn has been accused of failing to adapt and "stealing" jobs reserved for "real Americans." In crowded cities, where different ethnic groups occupied specific neighborhoods, fighting for "turf" was commonplace. Children suffered the most in many cases, lost in schools because they didn't speak English, left unsupervised by parents who could barely make ends meet at dead-end jobs, and harassed by youths of other races and religions who resented them.

They found safety in numbers—in street gangs.

The first gangs initially fought in self-defense, then for a sense of ethnic pride. Jobless and poorly educated, they soon turned to lives of crime: shoplifting, burglary, "protection" rackets, small-time gambling. Some specialized in particular crimes, ranging from petty theft and hijacking to contract murder. In the

1860s, New York's Irish Whyos gang offered a menu for potential customers:

Punching — $2
Both eyes blacked — $4
Nose and jaw broken — $10
Jacked [knocked] out — $15
Ear chewed off — $15
Leg or arm broken — $19
Shot in leg — $25
Stabbing — $25
The Big Job [murder] — $100[1]

## ⚲ FIVE POINTS

New York City's "Five Points" district—vividly depicted in the film *Gangs of New York* (2002)—was named for the intersection where five streets—Anthony, Cross, Little Water, Mulberry, and Orange—came together at Paradise Square. Despite that name, there was no hint of paradise to be found in the grim neighborhood. Already a filthy slum in the 1820s, 40 years later the area boasted 270 saloons, plus many gambling dens, houses of prostitution, and "grocery" stores that sold more liquor than food.

Five Points quickly became a breeding ground for gangs, including the Whyos, the Dead Rabbits, and the 1,500-member Five Points Gang, which was led by an Italian immigrant, Paolo Vaccarelli, who adopted the name "Paul Kelly" in order to pass as an Irishman. An ex-boxer, Kelly spoke four languages, dressed in high style, and forged alliances between his gang and New York City's most powerful leaders.

Other Five Points gangsters destined for ill-gotten riches and fame included Johnny "The Brain" Torrio, Al "Scarface" Capone, Charles "Lucky" Luciano, and Frankie Yale. Under Kelly's leadership, they fought epic battles with rival gangs, rigged elections for Tammany Hall, and paved the way for a new generation of organized crime in America.

By 1915, as the First World War raged in Europe and Africa, crime in Five Points began to decline. Ironically, the area had spawned so many criminals that they ran out of customers and

New York City was a haven for gangs in the late nineteenth century. The Five Points Gang alone boasted 1,500 members, battling in the streets with rivals that included the Plug Uglies, the Chichesters, the Eastmans, the Roach Guards, and the Dead Rabbits (who charged into combat with rabbits impaled on crude spears). One afternoon in August 1903, the Eastmans and Five Pointers fought for several hours, leaving three men dead and seven others shot, while the authorities were powerless to intervene.

Gangs of such size soon learned to use their influence, bribing corrupt police to overlook their crimes, and joining forces with New York's Tammany Hall and other political machines to rig

things to steal. Over the next five years, the boldest graduates of Five Points sought out greater opportunities. Paul Kelly organized illegal rackets on New York's waterfront. Torrio and Capone moved to Chicago, where they dominated criminal activities during the Roaring Twenties. Yale led New York's Mafia until his murder in 1928, while Luciano became the most powerful of all, acclaimed as "Boss of Bosses" for Italian gangs in the United States.

Artist's rendering of the Five Points in 1827. The area was known for gang activity, gambling, and prostitution. *Bettmann/Corbis* elections. Gangs in various neighborhoods were paid to deliver votes on demand, and their people voted as they were ordered—or else. In return, the hoodlums won friends in high places; politicians and judges protected their illegal enterprises for a share of the profits. By the early 1900s, cities such as New York, Chicago, Philadelphia, Kansas City, and New Orleans were largely controlled by a union of underworld thugs and greedy "public servants."

The underworld and government began to merge.

## THE WILD FRONTIER

Meanwhile, farther west, a different breed of gangsters challenged civilized society. Instead of terrorizing city ghettos, these men rode far and wide on horseback, stealing livestock, robbing travelers, and fighting range wars for whichever side offered the highest pay. Unlike their urban counterparts, western outlaws rarely formed close ties with government leaders, but police and courts were few and far between. Escape across the border to another state, or into Mexico, protected roaming outlaws from arrest.

As their environment was different from that of city gangs, so western outlaws differed, too, in other ways. Some of the most infamous gangs were family affairs, brothers and cousins bound by blood as much as greed. Many were veterans of the Civil War, especially in "Bleeding Kansas" and Missouri, where the battle over slavery began in 1856, five years before the shelling of Fort Sumter. Their experiences during the conflict had left them bitter and well versed in violence. Missouri spawned so many outlaw gangs after the War Between the States that it was nicknamed the "Mother of Bandits."

Criminals on the frontier found different paths to easy loot. Indiana's Reno brothers "invented" train robbery in October 1866, stealing some $160,000 ($1.6 million at modern exchange rates) before Pinkerton detectives and vigilante lynch mobs ended their career two years later. Missouri's James-Younger gang, another band of brothers, pioneered daylight bank robbery in February 1866 and kept it up for a decade, until most of its members were killed or captured at Northfield, Minnesota. The Dalton brothers, cousins of the Youngers, carried on the family tradition until 1892, when armed townspeople spoiled their plan to rob two banks at once in Coffeyville, Kansas, by killing or capturing most of the gang.

The Wild West gangs were small compared to those of New York City and Chicago, loosely-knit, and poorly suited for survival in a country where the open range was shrinking, and where cities were growing and becoming linked by new means of communication such as the telegraph and telephone. Butch Cassidy's "Wild Bunch" lasted until the early 1900s, when Butch and Harry Longabaugh—the "Sundance Kid"—fled to Bolivia, where even there the long arm of the law reached out to strike them down, and they were reportedly killed by local authorities.

Meanwhile, in U.S. cities, gangs were growing ever larger and more powerful.

## THE BLACK HAND

Some gangs were already well organized on foreign soil, before they came to the United States. Italy, for example, had been victimized for many years by criminal gangs including the Sicilian Mafia, the Camorra (active in Naples since 1735), and the 'Ndrangheta (based in Calabria). While such groups recruited only a small minority of Italians, their bribery and violence made them powerful. And when a flood of honest, hard-working Italians came to America in the late nineteenth century, some criminals came with them.

Once they landed in the States, those thugs resumed the same activities they had favored at home. Many practiced extortion—threatening demands for money or favors—against their fellow countrymen. Commonly, gangsters delivered a note to some businessman or celebrity, demanding payment under threat of death. Those notes were signed with the mark of a hand in black ink. Victims who ignored the threats were murdered, saw their children kidnapped, or their shops and homes destroyed by bombs.

No single "Black Hand" gang ever existed in America. The practice spread from New York to Chicago and a host of other cities where Italian immigrants had settled. Hundreds of victims died or suffered injury when they refused to pay. One Chicago Black Hander, a still-unknown terrorist nicknamed the "Shotgun Man," killed 15 victims during 1911–12. In New York, Ignazio "Lupo the Wolf" Saietta killed at least 60 men at his "murder stable" on East

107th Street before he was jailed in 1910 for printing counterfeit money.

American police had little luck in fighting Black Hand gangs. Most officers spoke no Italian, and the immigrants who suffered most from Black Hand crimes had learned to fear corrupt police in their homeland, a habit that was hard to break in U.S. cities where gangsters and dishonest law enforcement officers worked hand-in-hand.

One detective who fought the Black Hand gangs effectively was Giuseppe Petrosino, himself an immigrant who came to the United States at age 13 and joined New York City's police department 10 years later, in 1883. Petrosino hated gangsters and arrested hundreds, helping to deport some who were fugitives wanted for crimes in Italy. In early 1909, he went to Sicily, where he collected names of many immigrant gang members, but gunmen ambushed Petrosino in Palermo, killing him before he could use the list in New York.

## MOB RULE IN NEW ORLEANS

Police Chief David Hennessy, of New Orleans, also lost his life to gangsters. In 1890, two Sicilian crime families—the Matrangas and the Provenzanos—fought for control of the New Orleans waterfront, an area with many opportunities for theft and smuggling. Members of the Matranga gang believed that Chief Hennessy supported their rivals in that struggle. True or not, that belief prompted gunmen to kill Hennessy near his home on October 15.

A grand jury indicted 19 suspected gangsters, nine of whom faced trial in March 1891. On March 19, jurors acquitted six defendants, failing to reach verdicts on the other three. Rumors spread through New Orleans that the jury had been bribed, and witnesses intimidated. That afternoon an angry, vigilante mob of several thousand stormed the city jail and murdered 11 men suspected in Hennessey's case.

That lynching damaged relations between Italy and the United States. Rome withdrew its ambassador from Washington, D.C., and demanded payment of damages for the murders. Congress later paid $25,000 to relatives of the New Orleans victims, thereby settling the case at last.

Despite that controversy, mob violence had little real impact on criminal gangs in New Orleans. The Matranga group won its battle with the Provenzanos, and a member of the family—Charles Matranga—ruled the city's Italian crime syndicate until his death in 1925.

By that time, gangs across the country had received an unexpected gift from Uncle Sam in the form of a new law that would make it possible for gangsters to increase their wealth and influence beyond their wildest dreams.

# Supply and Demand

Gangs get rich by meeting public demands for banned products and services. Throughout history, wherever rulers have outlawed some activity or substance, criminals have organized to furnish the forbidden at higher prices. Prohibition rarely succeeds, and it *always* helps gangs grow larger and stronger, as illustrated by two examples from American history.

## THE "NOBLE EXPERIMENT"

Throughout history, some members of society have opposed manufacture and consumption of intoxicating substances, based on a variety of moral, social, and economic arguments. Some of these people believe alcoholic drinks (or drugs) to be evil and think that if all such things were banned, families would be saved, disease and crime rates would drop, and less money would be spent on prisons and police.

In the United States before the 1940s, crusaders focused most of their anger on "Demon Rum"—a catchall name for any alcoholic beverage. During World War I and the "Red Scare" (fear of radical violence mirroring the Communist Russian Revolution) that followed (1915–19), some critics also noted that much of the liquor industry was run by "un-American" immigrants, thus adding racism to the religious and social debate. Nine states were already "dry" by 1913. Four years later, Congress passed the 18th constitutional amendment, which banned alcohol, and sent it to the states

Prohibition-era poster urging voters to protect children from the evils of alcohol. *David J. & Janice L. Frent Collection/Corbis*

for ratification The last of 36 required states approved the amendment in January 1919, and it took effect one year later, enforced by a federal law, called the Volstead Act, that punished violators with fines and prison terms.

Supporters called Prohibition a "noble experiment," but it failed from the start. Minutes after the new law took effect on January 16, 1920, Chicago gangsters stole two freight cars filled with whiskey valued at $100,000. Over the next 13 years, until the 21st Amendment repealed the 18th in December 1933, America witnessed hundreds of such hijackings of illegal liquor shipments from outside the country, along with the storing of homemade liquor and "medicinal" liquor from government warehouses, before Prohibition took effect. There were thousands of murders linked to the traffic in bootleg liquor. Corruption flourished nationwide among police and federal agents, judges, and politicians. Even President Warren Harding (1921–23) served liquor in the White House, though he had supported Prohibition as a U.S. Senator.

Studies later proved that Prohibition's supporters had been wrong in most of their predictions. Alcohol consumption *increased* in America after liquor was banned, while speakeasies (illegal saloons) outnumbered former legal taverns roughly 10-to-1. Police arrested *more* people than ever before, though rarely touching wealthy gangsters who bribed them. Murder rates exploded in cities like Chicago, Detroit, and New York, where powerful gangs fought for control of the booze trade. Chicago alone recorded 627 gangland murders during 1920–33, while other victims simply disappeared on "one-way rides."

The problem, as crusaders quickly learned, was that many people who supported Prohibition publicly refused to give up their private pleasures. They paid lip service to the cause, and then went about their business as before.

That point was demonstrated by the new law's loophole for medical and religious use of alcohol. American doctors earned an estimated $40 million writing bogus liquor prescriptions for thirsty patients during 1920–28. Meanwhile, sales of sacramental wine increased from 2.1 million gallons in 1922 to 2.9 million gallons in 1924—a huge jump not reflected in higher church membership figures.

In short, Americans wanted to drink, and they needed someone to help quench that thirst.

## GETTING ORGANIZED

Every major American city had active criminal gangs by the time Prohibition became national law. Those in states like Michigan, which went dry before 1920, were already smuggling "alky" or making their own in illegal breweries and distilleries. Soon, fleets of ships established a thriving "Rum Row" off the Atlantic coast, unloading cargoes of Canadian or European alcohol beyond the 12-mile limit of U.S. jurisdiction, rushing the product ashore on speedboats with well-armed crews.

### ☌ AGAINST THE WALL

Chicago gangsters killed at least 627 persons during the Windy City's liquor wars of 1920–33. The most infamous killing occurred on February 14, 1929—St. Valentine's Day—when gunmen disguised as police killed six members of the North Side Gang and a visiting doctor in a garage on North Clark Street. The victims were lined up against a brick wall, then sprayed with machine-gun and shotgun fire at close range. North Side leader George "Bugs" Moran arrived late, and so escaped the massacre. While most observers blamed rival gang leader Al Capone for the killings, the crime remains officially unsolved.

Police *did* trace one of the massacre weapons, however, through microscopic examination. This type of examination reveals unique marks left by any given gun on every bullet it fires. Those marks on bullets from a crime scene can be matched to others test-fired from a suspect weapon to identify the gun(s) used in a crime.

Authorities found one of the Chicago massacre machine guns in December 1929 when they arrested gangster Fred "Killer" Burke for killing a Michigan policeman. Although the gun was definitely used on St. Valentine's Day, detectives could not prove that Burke participated in the slaughter. He received a life term for the Michigan slaying and later died in prison.

Today, many ballistics matches are made through computerized databases. The FBI premiered a database network called DRUGFIRE, which compared ballistics markings on bullets *and* other markings left by guns on their spent cartridge cases. The Bureau of Alcohol, Tobacco, Firearms and Explosives (ATF) operates a similar database

Competition for liquor territories soon produced bloodshed between rival gangs. Chicago recorded its first gangland murder of the dry era on February 2, 1920. Three months later, gunmen killed the city's top gangster, "Big Jim" Colosimo, and the booze wars began in earnest. Across the country, in cities from New York and Miami to Los Angeles and San Francisco, it was much the same.

Some gangsters kill because they are violent by nature; others kill because they cannot settle criminal disputes in court, by peaceful means. Soon, wise gangsters realized that public murders—like

known as IBIS (the integrated ballistics identification system), which has replaced DRUGFIRE. IBIS software has two separate identification programs, Bulletproof (for comparison of bullets) and Brasscatcher (for matching cartridge cases).

As with all other forensic evidence—DNA, fingerprints, bite marks—ballistics and firearms identification experts can only link unsolved crimes if they have a weapon in their hands to study. And even then, a gun without known users will not solve a crime.

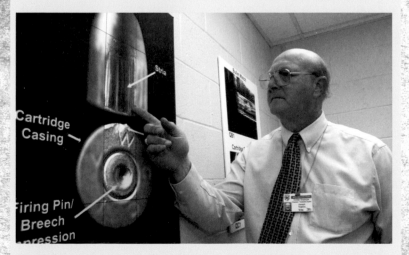

A firearms examiner points to the area on a bullet that will be utilized by the Integrated Ballistics Identification System, an advanced tool used to help identify the gun that a bullet was fired from. *AP Photo/Gail Burton*

cheap homemade booze that was toxic and blinded or killed those who drank it—was bad for business. They began to cooperate, negotiating disagreements and assigning neighborhoods (or larger territories) to specific gangs.

The first such syndicate, known as the "Big Seven," was created in 1926. Its leaders included top gangsters from New York City, Philadelphia, New Jersey, and Boston. Membership was not confined to any single ethnic group. Three years later, in May 1929, gang leaders from Chicago, Cleveland, Detroit, and Kansas City joined members of the Big Seven for a three-day underworld convention in Atlantic City, New Jersey, drawing up the rough blueprint for a nationwide crime syndicate. Young Mafia members, led by New York's Lucky Luciano, killed off their old-fashioned bosses in 1930–31, paving the way for better relations with gangsters of other races. More meetings during 1932–34 ironed out the details of a crime network that remains active and powerful today.

So it was that Prohibition made gangs stronger than ever before, while increasing corruption in government and law enforcement. By the time America turned "wet" again, on December 5, 1933, the noble experiment had spawned a monster.

And the crusaders still had not learned their lesson.

## DRUG WARS

Harry Anslinger (1892–1975) served as a Prohibition enforcement officer until August 1930, when President Franklin Roosevelt chose him to lead the new Federal Bureau of Narcotics (FBN). Anslinger held that post for 32 years, during which time he fought to ban all recreational drugs from the country. His belief that drugs were evil may have been sincere. It also helped Anslinger get more money and more agents for the FBN each year, competing with J. Edgar Hoover's FBI.

Anslinger's first target was marijuana. He claimed that smokers of the "demon weed" were often violent, responsible for brutal murders and a host of other crimes. His publicity campaign, including the film *Reefer Madness* (1936), persuaded Congress to ban marijuana in 1937, followed by an ever-growing list of state and federal laws restricting other drugs. Each new law made more work for Anslinger's FBN and created new opportunities for drug-dealing gangsters.

In 1971, President Richard Nixon branded illegal drugs "America's public enemy number one" and created a new Drug Enforcement Administration (DEA) to lead an "all-out offensive" against drug traffickers. Ten years later, with drug sales higher than ever, President Ronald Reagan declared a federal "war on drugs." In 1988, Reagan created the Office of National Drug Control Policy, whose leader is commonly called the "Drug Czar."

Tough talk accomplished little. Meanwhile, drug-trafficking gangs earned billions of dollars, spent millions on bribes, and committed thousands of murders worldwide. Colombia, source for much of the cocaine sold in America, averaged 30,000 murders and 75 political assassinations per year in the 1980s and 1990s.

Multi-agency task forces, combining officers from two or more different law enforcement agencies, are frequently used to combat drug-smuggling syndicates. In the year 2003 alone, 5,959 American police officers participated in task force investigations, involving 23 percent of all law enforcement agencies in the United States. Cooperation of this kind is helpful, since most drug offenses are defined by state and local statutes.

More than 80 percent of all drug arrests and convictions in America involve the offense of possession, while fewer than one-fifth involve smuggling or manufacture of illegal drugs. In 1987, drug offenses produced 7.4 percent of all American arrests, nearly doubling to 13.1 percent by 2005. Critics of current drug policy suggest that those statistics—and the high percentage of arrests for simple possession—indicate time and effort wasted arresting small-time drug users, rather than wealthy drug producers and drug traffickers.

It is true that drug enforcement creates some impressive statistics. State and federal officers seized 11.4 million pounds of illegal drugs during 2000–03. In 2003 alone, raiders captured 420 drug labs and destroyed 3.4 million marijuana plants at 34,362 different locations. In 2005, police jailed 1,846,400 persons for various drug offenses.

Trends in drug abuse change over time. Between 1987 and 1995, a majority of drug arrests involved cocaine and heroin. Since 1996, according to the FBI, arrests involving marijuana have surpassed all other types of drugs. In 2003, reports from the Federal-Wide Drug Seizure System (including reports from the FBI, DEA, Customs Service, Border Patrol, and Coast Guard) included seizures of

5,643 pounds of heroin, 245,499 pounds of cocaine, and 2,700,282 pounds of marijuana. In the same year, authorities seized 420 illegal drug labs, 409 of which produced methamphetamines. Other seizures for the year included 4,176 weapons and various assets valued at $25.1 million.

Still, those victories are small. Authorities admit that they find less than 10 percent of all illegal drugs in the United States. Most persons arrested are held for possession of small quantities, while large dealers often escape. Their prosecution and incarceration for minor offenses cost billions of dollars each year.

And the gangsters get richer each day.

## GOLD RUSH IN GANGLAND

As with bootleg booze in "dry" America, illegal drugs are a goldmine for gangsters. Public tastes change over time, along with emphasis on drug enforcement, but gangs provide whatever chemicals their customers demand.

According to the DEA, most drug arrests between 1987 and 1995 involved cocaine and heroin. Both drugs are still widely available today, but, as mentioned earlier, marijuana arrests have exceeded all others since 1996.

Nationwide, as in the 1920s, various gangs dominate different drug markets. Inner-city gangs control most of the traffic in "crack" cocaine, while Latin American syndicates smuggle cocaine in powder form. Asian, Italian, and Mexican gangs import most of America's heroin. Motorcycle gangs dominate manufacture and sale of illegal amphetamines. When their interests conflict, bloody gang wars erupt, often with innocent bystanders caught in the crossfire.

## LEARNING FROM HISTORY

In his *Philosophy of History*, German author Georg Hegel (1770–1831) wrote: "Peoples and governments never have learned anything from history, or acted on principles deduced from it." In other words, people seldom learn from their mistakes.

Such is the case with prohibition.

In 1920 the government banned alcohol to "save" society from crime, corruption, and disease. That effort failed, transforming anyone who drank or sold liquor into a criminal, tempting police, judges, and politicians to accept more bribes. From the White House to patrolmen on the beat, few managed to resist.

Today, the "war on drugs" fills jails, claims lives, and corrupts authority—just as the war on liquor did more than 70 years ago. Gangs profit from the ban, as they have always done.

## ⚲ WHAT "WAR ON DRUGS"?

Government officials, including the U.S. President, are sometimes inconsistent in their efforts to control illegal drugs. President Ronald Reagan announced a federal "war on drugs" in January 1982, placing then Vice President George H.W. Bush in charge of the effort. Around the same time, however, Reagan also slashed funding for organized-crime investigations by the FBI, DEA, Coast Guard, Internal Revenue Service, and other federal agencies. Critics in law enforcement noted Reagan's longtime friendship with alleged members of organized crime and corrupt labor unions,

*(continues)*

President Reagan gestures during a 1987 news conference regarding the Iran-Contra scandal. Reagan denied all knowledge of illegal activities and was never implicated by legal officials. *AP Photo/Dennis Cook*

*(continued)*

dating from the 1930s and continuing through his terms as gover-nor of California (1967–74) and his two presidential campaigns.

In November 1986, journalists revealed that members of the Reagan administration armed Nicaragua's right-wing "Contra" guerrillas in violation of federal law *and* engaged in cocaine sales to raise money for Contra terrorist campaigns.

The Iran-Contra scandal—so called because it also included illegal arms sales to Iran—soured Reagan's second term as presi-dent. On November 6, 1986, Reagan publicly denied reports of the scandal, then announced one week later that the news stories were true. A U.S. Senate report in 1988 documented participation of federal officials in cocaine transactions for the Contras. It was never proven that Reagan, who denied knowledge of the illegal activities, was aware of them before the scandal broke. Six mem-bers of the Reagan-Bush administration were convicted for their roles in the scandal, but President George H. W. Bush pardoned all of them before leaving office in January 1993.

What is being done wrong?

Some prohibition critics focus on the problems of enforcement, while others take aim at the policy itself. Enforcement critics note that most of those arrested are small-time offenders, often poor, and frequently members of racial minorities. When wealthy Caucasian offenders *are* charged, they often escape with a fine and probation instead of jail time. Meanwhile, the prosecution and imprisonment of petty drug offenders costs billions of dollars, which, critics say, could be better used against violent predators and high-level white-collar criminals.

Critics of policy attack the prohibition concept on its merits, maintaining that "wars" against intoxicating substances are inef-fective, increase crime, and enrich gangsters, while eroding personal freedom. The war on drugs began with a $350 million budget in 1971, but cost $20 billion in 2006, after 35 years of failure. That money, they contend, would be better spent solving other problems in modern America. Critics also note the inconsistency of banning certain drugs while other legal substances—alcohol and nicotine—are known to cause thousands of deaths every year.

In short, critics suggest that ending prohibition would reduce crime, save billions of dollars, and rob organized gangs of their most lucrative products. It may even *reduce* drug addiction, as revealed by studies in the Netherlands after drugs were decriminalized.

Today, drug crimes include burglaries and holdups that users commit to get money to buy drugs, as well as shootings and murders committed by drug gangs. Special techniques in fighting drug dealers include undercover investigations and analysis of seized drugs to determine their source and identify suppliers. Packaging for illegal drugs is treated like any other evidence and processed for latent prints and DNA in an effort to identify those involved. The battle against drug-related gangs continues.

# Public Enemies
# and Holdup Gangs

Americans love to rate celebrities. Who is the most beautiful? Who is the richest? Who has the most power in Hollywood?

People play the same game with notorious criminals. Which one is most dangerous? Who has the most dirty money hidden in offshore bank accounts? Who controls the most sluggers or hitmen? Which one has the strangest nickname?

Before Prohibition, when wealthy bootleggers became celebrities on par with movie stars, there was no system of ranking criminals, except by the size of rewards offered for their capture. That changed on April 28, 1930, when the Chicago Crime Commission (a private group with no police powers) published its first list of public enemies living in the Windy City.

All 28 men on the list were bootleggers. Mobster "Scarface" Al Capone ranked No. 1, with his brother Ralph at No. 3. Roughly half of the remaining 26 were members of Capone's gang, while the rest were enemies who fought against Capone in Chicago's long-running beer wars.

Four years later, leaders of the Chicago Crime Commission suggested that the U.S. Justice Department create its own public enemies list. J. Edgar Hoover (1895–1972), longtime boss of the Federal Bureau of Investigation (FBI), refused to participate, but Attorney General Homer Cummings announced a list of federal public enemies on June 22, 1934.

Unlike the Chicago list, the federal dishonor roll completely ignored leaders of organized crime. Instead, it listed 20 old-fashioned bandits and two women known to travel with John Dillinger's

Al Capone was at the top of the list released by the Chicago Crime Commission ranking the most wanted outlaws living in the city. The list, released on April 28, 1930, was the first of its kind. *AP Photo/file*

bank-robbing gang. Dillinger himself ranked No. 1, while George "Baby Face" Nelson trailed in the list at No. 21.

The difference in choosing public enemies highlights a gap between state and federal gang-busting efforts. While Chicago authorities tried to tackle large crime syndicates (with help from federal tax agents), Hoover's FBI would publicly deny the existence of organized crime until the early 1960s.

## WHERE THE MONEY IS

American bandits have always robbed banks. When a reporter asked veteran stickup artist Willie Sutton why *he* robbed banks, Sutton allegedly replied, "That's where the money is." Before his death in 1980, Sutton flatly denied making any such statement, but in any case, it captures the essence of armed robbery.

Banks *are* where the money is.

Before the Civil War (1861–65), American bank robbers were actually burglars who broke in after closing time and looted vaults or safe-deposit boxes overnight. The James-Younger gang staged America's first daylight bank robbery at Liberty, Missouri, in February 1866. From there, the gang robbed other banks and also looted trains. The Dalton brothers, cousins of the Youngers, later picked up where their relatives left off, continuing the family tradition until they were slaughtered at Coffeyville, Kansas, while robbing two banks at once on October 15, 1892.

Bank robbery did not die with the Daltons; quite the reverse, in fact. America's farm depression of the 1920s, followed by the stock market crash of 1929 and the Great Depression of 1930–41, encouraged certain reckless men (and a few female "gun molls") to loot the banks that had foreclosed on their mortgages, leaving them homeless and broke.

Thus a new generation of bandits was born, traveling in cars rather than on horseback, armed with machine guns and automatic rifles instead of six-shooters. Their heyday would be brief but violent, and it would change American law enforcement forever.

## WANTED—DEAD!

Some bank-robbing gangs were more successful than others. The four Newton brothers, with various friends, robbed at least 80 banks between 1918 and 1924. Many of their holdups were in Texas, which also produced other infamous bandits such as Clyde Barrow and Bonnie Parker (subjects of the 1967 film *Bonnie and Clyde*).

By 1928 leaders of the Texas Bankers Association were so upset by unsolved holdups that they posted the following notice in every bank statewide:

### REWARD

### $5,000 FOR DEAD BANK ROBBERS

### NOT ONE CENT FOR LIVE ONES

That incitement to kill offenders who would not face the death penalty if captured alive caused national outrage. Bad publicity forced a recall of the posters, which were rewritten to offer rewards for bank robbers caught "Dead or Alive." The spirit of the offer would prevail, however, and several famous bandits would be shot on sight over the next few years, even when they were found unarmed.

At the beginning of the Great Depression, robbing banks was not a federal crime. Bandits could rob a bank in Texas, then flee into Arkansas or Oklahoma and relax with no fear of arrest. It would require a massacre to close that loophole in the law and give J. Edgar Hoover's FBI a chance to launch its famous War on Crime.

## MURDER IN TOM'S TOWN

Frank "Jelly" Nash (1887–1933) was an old-fashioned outlaw, arrested for burglary six times in the last half of 1911 alone. He was also a bank and train robber, a quick-trigger killer, and friend to some of the era's most notorious criminals. In March 1924, Nash received a 25-year prison term for robbing the U.S. Mail. He served a little over six years, then escaped from Leavenworth Prison in October 1930 and joined another bank-robbing gang.

Nash robbed at least six more banks, stealing an estimated $494,000 in cash and bonds between April 1931 and April 1933. In June 1933, FBI agents traced him to Hot Springs, Arkansas, one of several "open cities" where corrupt police and politicians sheltered fugitives for a price.

While Nash's holdups were state offenses, Leavenworth was a federal prison, and his escape permitted FBI agents to arrest him. They grabbed Nash in Hot Springs on June 16, and put him aboard a train back to Leavenworth.

But he never made it.

Moments after Nash's arrest, his friends telephoned gangsters in Kansas City—known as "Tom's Town" in those days, since nothing happened without permission from crooked political boss Tom Pendergast. The call alerted friends of Nash to his arrival time at

## ♀ THE WILD BUNCH

Between Jesse James and John Dillinger, America's most famous outlaw was probably Robert LeRoy Parker, better known as Butch Cassidy. Born in 1867, Cassidy logged his first arrest at 13 and spent the rest of his life as an outlaw. He led a bank- and train-robbing gang that was nicknamed the Wild Bunch, operating from a rocky Wyoming hideout called Hole-in-the-Wall. Aside from

*(continues)*

A portrait of the Wild Bunch. Seated (left to right): "Sundance Kid," Ben Kilpatrick, and Butch Cassidy. Standing (left to right): Bill Carver, Kid Curry. *Bettmann/Corbis*

*(continued)*

Cassidy, the gang's most notorious member was Harry Long-abaugh, better known as the Sundance Kid.

Between 1896 and 1900, the Wild Bunch rode and robbed at will over half a dozen states, eluding sheriffs, lynch mobs, Pinkerton detectives, and Wells Fargo agents. Pressure from law enforcement—including posses that traveled by train, with their horses saddled and ready to ride if the bandits struck—caused gang members to scatter in the early 1900s, most of them shot, hanged, or imprisoned. The last known member, Ben Kilpatrick, was killed by railroad express guards in March 1912.

Butch and Sundance beat the heat by fleeing to New York, then moved on to South America. They traveled with Longabaugh's girlfriend to divert suspicion, but their bad habits resurfaced in Argentina and Bolivia, where they robbed more banks during 1905–08. In early 1909, soldiers reportedly cornered the bandits at San Vicente, Bolivia, and killed them in a shootout—but again, as with Dillinger, stories persist that one or both survived.

Whether those tales are true or not, their memory lives on. Two Hollywood films, both released in 1969, portrayed the gang in very different ways. *Butch Cassidy and the Sundance Kid*, starring Paul Newman and Robert Redford in the title roles, downplayed the gang's violence and added a comic touch, winning an Academy Award for best screenplay.

Director Sam Peckinpah took a different approach with *The Wild Bunch*, producing the first "splatter" Western with a bloody tale of aging badmen robbing and dying on the Mexican border in 1913. In Brian Fox's 1969 novel, based on the movie script and with the same title, gang members regret not following Butch and Sundance to Bolivia.

Kansas City's Union Station, where he would be met by more police and FBI agents with cars, to drive him back to Leavenworth.

Nash's train arrived at 7 a.m. on June 17. Seven lawmen walked Nash toward two waiting cars—and what happened next changed American history.

As the men reached their vehicles, an uncertain number of gangsters appeared, armed with machine guns and pistols. Someone fired a shot, and when the gunsmoke cleared, three policemen and one FBI agent lay dead, with two more agents wounded. Nash also died from gunshots to the head.

The "Kansas City Massacre" infuriated most Americans. In May 1934, Congress passed new laws expanding the FBI's powers and

Charles "Pretty Boy" Floyd in a 1932 photo. Floyd denied involvement in the "Kansas City Massacre." *AP Photo/file*

making it a federal crime to rob banks insured by the U.S. government. That law would launch a bloody three-year war against bank-robbing gangs—and also, incidentally, promote J. Edgar Hoover to the status of a national celebrity.

After several false starts, FBI agents identified the Kansas City killers as Vernon Miller (a war-hero sheriff turned bandit and hit-man), Charles "Pretty Boy" Floyd (an Oklahoma outlaw linked to several murders), and Floyd's alcoholic partner Adam Richetti. Author Robert Unger disputes those selections in his book *The Union Station Massacre* (1997), but no one questioned Hoover at the time.

Fellow gangsters killed Vern Miller in November 1933, but 11 months later, FBI agents traced Floyd and Richetti to Ohio; they arrested Richetti and killed Floyd. With his dying breath, Floyd denied participation in the Kansas City murders. Jurors convicted Richetti and he was executed in October 1938.

## "DON'T SHOOT, G-MEN!"

George "Machine Gun" Kelly launched his criminal career as a bootlegger, then graduated to bank jobs with Frank Nash and other stickup artists in the early 1930s. On July 22, 1933, with partner Albert Bates, Kelly kidnapped oilman Charles Urschel from his home in Oklahoma City. The gangsters held Urschel for nine days in Texas, then released him after collecting a $200,000 ransom.

Sadly for Kelly and Bates, Congress had made interstate kidnapping a federal crime in 1932, after the infant son of hero-pilot Charles Lindbergh was kidnapped and killed in New Jersey. The Lindbergh Law allowed FBI agents to join in the manhunt for Urschel's abductors. Detectives in Dallas were friendly with George Kelly's wife and took note when she started flashing money after Urschel's ransom was paid. Soon, they found the ranch where Urschel had been held.

According to popular legend, the FBI tracked Kelly to Memphis, Tennessee, and arrested him there on September 26, 1933, frightening him so badly that he cowered on his knees, crying, "Don't shoot, G-men!" (The *G* stood for government.) In fact, he was captured by Memphis police and said no such thing, but the myth lives on. FBI agents are still known as G-men—or G-women—today.

Kelly, his wife Katherine, and Al Bates received life prison terms for the Urschel kidnapping. Several members of Katherine's family also served time as accomplices to the crime.

## SEE JOHNNY RUN

John Herbert Dillinger (1903–34) ranks as the most famous American bandit since Jesse James (1848–82). Like James, he fired the imagination of reporters and average citizens, thousands of whom mourned his death. And like James, he would inspire reports that he survived his final showdown with authorities, leaving a "double" in his grave.

Dillinger was born in Indiana and joined the Navy at age 20, but deserted after a few months at sea. In September 1924, he joined an older man in a bungled robbery and was arrested. Pleading guilty on his lawyer's advice, he received a prison term of two to 20 years that left him angry and bitter.

In prison, Dillinger made friends with various hard-core outlaws and promised to help them escape when he was paroled in May 1933. To finance that breakout, he joined a bank-robbing gang and pulled a dozen holdups that summer. In September 1933, he smuggled pistols into Indiana's state prison for his friends. Ten of them escaped on September 26.

But by then, Dillinger was in jail.

Ohio police caught him four days before the jailbreak, holding him at a jail in Lima, Ohio, on robbery charges. His fugitive friends returned the favor on October 12, freeing Dillinger and killing Sheriff Jesse Sarber in the process.

A spree of daring holdups followed across the Midwest. Dillinger's gang seemed to be everywhere at once. When they took a break in Arizona, in January 1934, sharp-eyed police caught Dillinger and three companions. Dillinger faced murder charges in Indiana for shooting a policeman, but he carved a wooden gun and escaped once again.

Forming a new gang, Dillinger soon pulled more holdups. FBI agents joined the chase and cornered the gang at a Wisconsin lodge on April 22. The raid went badly, claiming two innocent lives, while the gangsters escaped.

John Dillinger, center, is handcuffed and guarded in court in February 1934. Dillinger was charged with the killing of a police officer in Indiana. *AP Photo*

G-men got lucky in July 1934 when a prostitute facing deportation to Europe betrayed Dillinger in Chicago. FBI agents waited outside a local theater on July 22, and shot Dillinger as he emerged.

Or did they?

In 1970 author Jay Nash (*Dillinger: Dead of Alive?*) claimed that Mafia leaders helped Dillinger fake his own death, while G-men killed an innocent "patsy." Few historians support that theory.

## OLD CRIMES, NEW LAWS

Prior to the 1930s, most law enforcement was a state or local matter. Authority of federal agents was generally restricted to crimes committed on government property, thefts from U.S. mail, and similar crimes that directly involved the federal government. As in the nineteenth century, criminal gangs could rob, kidnap, or murder in one state, then escape prosecution by fleeing to another, where police had no reason to hunt them.

A series of sensational crimes in the early 1930s, starting with the 1932 kidnap-murder of Charles Lindbergh Jr. and the 1933 Kansas City massacre, prompted Congress to pass a series of new laws applying federal jurisdiction to formerly local offenses. The Lindbergh Law of 1932 made it a federal crime to carry kidnap victims across state lines, while a 1933 amendment allowed execution of interstate kidnappers who harmed their victims. Other laws penalized bandits who robbed federally insured banks, killed or injured federal agents, crossed state lines to avoid arrest or imprisonment, or armed themselves with unregistered "gangster weapons" (i.e., machine guns, sawed-off shotguns, and "silencers").

Today's gangs are growing and becoming more sophisticated. Legislators and law enforcement authorities must look to new techniques and laws to combat gang crimes.

# Hell on Wheels

Police got the call on April 8, 2006. A farmer in Shedden, Ontario, had found two cars and a tow truck with a third car attached to it parked on his land without permission. When he looked into one of the cars, the farmer saw two bodies slumped in the backseat.

Officers soon found six more corpses crammed into the vehicles. All were male and all had died from close-range gunshot wounds. Driver's licenses and fingerprints identified the victims. All came from Toronto or its suburbs and were members of the Bandidos Motorcycle Club, described by police as a criminal gang. They ranged in age from 30 to 52 years old.

Suspicion focused first on a rival "club," the Hells Angels, but spokesmen for that organization denied any link to the mass murder. On April 10, police arrested five Bandidos, including longtime biker Wayne Kellestine, formerly a member of the Annihilators, who lived a few miles from the crime scene.

Kellestine had been charged with shooting another biker in 1991, but charges were dropped. Eight years later, gunmen sent to kill him by a rival gang fired into the wrong car. He had also served time for drug and weapons offenses. Prosecutors say Kellestine ordered the deaths of his fellow club members because they ignored orders to join in a gang "run" (ride) to Winnipeg. Police also say that large quantities of cocaine and other drugs were stolen from the victims during the murders.

The Canadian massacre offered a glimpse inside a strange subculture few "normal" people ever see: the weird and violent world of outlaw motorcycle gangs.

Bandidos biker gang jackets on display at a police news conference on the murder of eight members of the gang in Ontario in April 2006. *AP Photo/CP, John Woods*

## THE 1-PERCENTERS

Rowdy bikers have been tearing up the highways of America since 1946, when "Wino Willie" Forkner founded California's Boozefighter Motorcycle Club. On July 4, 1947, the Boozefighters and 4,000 other bikers ran wild through the streets of Hollister, California, leaving 50 persons injured and 100 in jail. Two months later, on Labor Day, 6,000 bikers staged a similar riot in Riverside, California.

Those incidents inspired America's first film about motorcycle gangs, *The Wild One* (1953), starring Marlon Brando and Lee Marvin as rival gang leaders. The riots also prompted spokesmen for the American Motorcycle Association to announce that 99 percent of all bikers are law-abiding citizens, while only 1 percent are "outlaws." Clubs like the Boozefighters happily accepted the outlaw label and began wearing "1%" patches on their jackets.

Outlaw bikers generally seem proud of their reputation for drunken, reckless behavior. (The Boozefighters described themselves, humorously, as "a drinking club with a motorcycle problem.") They often appear unwashed and ungroomed—though their motorcycles are spotless—and they decorate themselves with tattoos or patches designed to cause public outrage.

When pressed on the point, most 1-percenters will claim that their appearance and behavior simply represent an alternate lifestyle. They deny involvement in any serious crime, even when their records include long lists of felony convictions. "Gonzo" journalist Hunter Thompson supported that view of disorganized, fun-loving goons in his 1967 book *Hell's Angels*.

Police tell a very different story, describing the major outlaw biker gangs as a subset of organized crime, dealing drugs, weapons, and other contraband on an international scale and earning billions of dollars each year.

## THE BIG FOUR

While dozens of 1 percent motorcycle gangs flourish worldwide, police mark four groups as the hands-down leaders in violent criminal activity. In order of creation, they include

■ The Outlaws Motorcycle Club, organized in 1935 in the Chicago suburb of McCook, Illinois. The group's membership dwindled during World War II, and club literature admits that its activities remained "limited" until 1950, when reorganization began in Chicago. The gang's present-day insignia, a skull with crossed pistons, was adopted in 1954. Present-day headquarters are located in Daytona Beach, Florida, while the gang claims 2,800 members in 200 chapters worldwide. Outlaws are bitter enemies of the Hells Angels, involved in a long-running war that has claimed hundreds of lives throughout the United States and Canada. Ninety-five victims died in Florida and North Carolina alone, during 1974–84. Member Harry Bowman earned a spot on the FBI's Ten Most Wanted list in 1998 as a fugitive on triple-murder charges. He is presently serving a life prison term.

■ The Hells Angels, founded in 1948 in Fontana, California. The group took its name from a 1930 war movie, *Hell's Angels*, but soon dropped the apostrophe. Most early members were young

## ♀ COLORS

Outlaw bikers are identified by their *colors*—gang emblems worn on the back of their jackets or vests. "Full-patch" members wear a club insignia with arched rockers above and below, bearing the gang's name and the name of their chapter's hometown. Probationary members generally wear a single rocker reading "Prospect." Other emblems worn by various bikers, either as patches or tattoos, include the following[1]:

*ADIOS* - Angels Die in Outlaw States (worn by Outlaws)
*AFFA* - Angels Forever, Forever Angels
*AFFL* - Alcohol Forever, Forever Loaded
*AHAMD* - All Hells Angels Must Die (worn by Outlaws)
*AOA* - American Outlaws Association, on patch with a hand making a rude gesture, the Outlaws' "answer" to the American Motorcycle Association
*BTBF* - Bikers Together, Bikers Forever
*Deguello* - "No quarter"; a pledge to violently resist arrest
*DFFL* - Dope Forever, Forever Loaded
*Filthy Few* - Patch awarded to Hells Angels who have killed for the gang
*HAMC* - Hells Angels Motorcycle Club
*LL* - Lounge Lizard, worn by Outlaws who have served prison time
*MC* - Motorcycle club
*Property Of...* - Worn by a gang's female associates, with the club's name included
*S* - Speed (amphetamines)
*\** - Tattooed between thumb and forefinger, one for each prison term served
*1%* - Designating a biker's "outlaw" status
*13* - From the 13th letter (M), for *marijuana*
*22* - Indicates a biker who has served prison time
*24* - Signifies drinking 24 beers in under 8 hours
*81* - HA, for Hells Angels (eighth and first letters)

veterans of World War II. During the Vietnam War, Hells Angels offered to fight as a unit in Southeast Asia (they were rejected) and clashed repeatedly with antiwar demonstrators. In 1969, Angels serving as security guards at a Rolling Stones concert in Altamont, California, killed a man who approached the stage

*88* - Heil Hitler (double H, the eighth letter)

*100% Pure* - Pure Caucasian (White Pride)

*187* - Murder (from the California penal code number)

*666* - Satan

*Clenched white fist* - White Power

*Clock face without hands* - Serving prison time

*Colored wings* - Patterned on pilots' wings, but in various colors denoting different sex acts

*Eight ball* - Bad luck

*Featherwood* - Worn by females to denote White Pride

*Lightning bolts* - Originally worn by Nazi SS members in Hitler's Germany, worn today by some bikers to symbolize White Power. When worn by Outlaws, the emblem denotes a member who has committed murder, attempted murder, or detonated a bomb in gang warfare.

*Peckerwood* - Worn by males to denote White Pride

*Spider web on shoulder or elbow* - Serving prison time

*Swastika* - White Power

*SWP* - Supreme White Power

*Tombstone with numbers* - Signifies number of years served in prison

*Tombstone with "R.I.P."* - Denotes the death of a friend

*Upside-down license plates* - Stolen from police vehicles or rival bikers

*Viking emblems or themes* - Nordic/white pride

*White Cross* - Worn as pin or earring, signifies a biker who has robbed a grave and wears the stolen item on his colors

Some motorcycle gangs also adopt mottos that express their view of life. The unofficial Hells Angels motto is "Three can keep a secret if two are dead." Bandidos proclaim that, "We are the people our parents warned us about." Outlaws warn outsiders: "God Forgives, Outlaws Don't."

with a gun. In 2006 the group sued Walt Disney studios to block release of a new film, *Wild Hogs,* which allegedly included an unflattering depiction of gang members. At press time for this book, there were some 2,000 Hells Angels in 235 chapters, spanning 22 countries worldwide.

■ The Pagans, founded in 1959, was the brainchild of Louis Dobkins, a biochemist at the National Institute of Health in Prince Georges County, Maryland. By 1968, it was the dominant East Coast motorcycle gang and retains its greatest strength in that region today. A war between the Pagans and the rival Warlocks claimed at least 15 lives in Pennsylvania during 1974–75. During the same period, Pennsylvania Pagans were suspected (but never charged) in the serial murders of six women and several Mafia-related bombings. Today, the gang has an estimated 900 members in 44 chapters.

■ The Bandidos, or Bandido Nation, founded in 1966 by Donald Eugene Chambers of Houston, Texas. Chambers later claimed that his inspiration for the club's insignia was TV's "Frito Bandito" (which Chambers misspelled), a cartoon character in commercials for Fritos corn chips. The gang has strong ties to organized crime and a record of deadly violence. Gang members wounded U.S. Attorney Jim Kerr of Texas in a 1978 machine-gun ambush, and they were also blamed for killing federal judge John Wood in May 1979. (Charles Harrelson, father of actor Woody Harrelson, received a life sentence as the shooter in that murder.) Police also suspect Bandidos in the 2004 murder of former world heavyweight boxing champion Robert Quiroga. Ranked as America's fastest-growing biker gang in 2006, the Bandidos have an estimated 600 members worldwide.

## CRIME, INTERNATIONAL

Police spokesmen claim that outlaw biker gangs dominate production and sales of crank or ice (crystal methamphetamine) in the United States, with lucrative sidelines in prostitution and strip clubs, gunrunning, and money laundering. Since the late 1960s, however, some of the larger gangs have established chapters in countries from Canada and Europe to Australia, New Zealand, and Thailand. FBI agents estimate that the Hells Angels alone earn $1 billion per year from various criminal activities.

Canada is the most active 1-percenter realm outside of the United States, with Hells Angels dominating the field. Bandidos gained entry by absorbing the homegrown Rock Machine gang, but they are still heavily outnumbered by Hells Angels. In the early 1980s, Canadian Angel Yves "Apache" Trudeau confessed to 46 murders, with victims including several fellow Hells Angels in Montreal. Angels killed several of their own in a "cleanup" of the Montreal North chapter in March 1985. Since 1994, biker wars in Quebec have produced more than 100 murders, 130 cases of arson, and 84 bombings. In July 2005, an Ontario judge branded the Hells Angels a criminal organization, under Canada's laws governing organized crime.

While England's Hells Angels seem mainly involved in underground music promotions, police also monitor gang participation in drug trafficking. Member William Anderson, convicted of smuggling cocaine in association with Colombian gangsters, later escaped from Sudbury prison.

Scandinavia witnessed a bloody war between Hells Angels and Bandidos during 1993–96. A sniper killed Bandidos leader Mikael Ljunggren in Sweden, and successor Uffe Larsen died in a machine-gun ambush at Copenhagen's airport. In October 1996, Bandidos fired a rocket into the Angels' Copenhagen clubhouse, killing two persons and wounding 19. When authorities threatened to pass new anti-gang laws in early 1997, leaders of both gangs appeared on television to announce a cease-fire.

Australia has banned the Hells Angels as a criminal organization, but the gang survives in covert competition with the Bandidos. In September 1984, a shootout between Bandidos and rival Commancheros at Milperra left seven dead and 21 wounded.

In nearby New Zealand, Hells Angels have skirmished with native bike clubs including the Road Knights and the Highway 61 gang, fighting for control of nationwide drug traffic.

## POLICING OUTLAW BIKERS

During the 1970s, American police identified nearly 900 outlaw motorcycle gangs nationwide, some—like the Big Four—with numerous local chapters. By the 1980s, FBI spokesmen recognized bikers as a top priority in organized crime investigations, second only to the Mafia or *Cosa Nostra*—but the close-knit nature of the gangs made prosecution difficult.

Since the mid-1980s agents of the FBI, the Drug Enforcement Administration, and the ATF have attacked outlaw biker gangs through a combination of traditional surveillance (court-ordered bugs and wiretaps) and infiltration by officers posing as bikers. In the 1990s, ATF agent William Queen penetrated the Mongols, a gang based in Los Angeles, and gathered evidence leading to 53 convictions. Jay Dobyns, another ATF agent who infiltrated the Arizona Hells Angels, later reported gang threats against his wife and children.

With information gathered from wiretaps and undercover agents, many outlaw bikers have been indicted on conspiracy and racketeering charges, with specific offenses including murder, drug trafficking, kidnapping, extortion, and attempted jury-tampering. Other countries, notably Canada and Australia, have used their immigration laws to bar American gang members from recruiting on foreign soil. While those actions disrupt some criminal operations, the wealthy gangs retain attorneys specializing in defense of organized-crime charges. Even conviction and imprisonment may serve outlaw bikers, as they coordinate drug sales and other activities with established prison gangs.

# Prison Gangs

On December 14, 2002, 30-year-old carnival worker Robert Maricle disappeared while visiting friends at an apartment complex in Salinas, California. Witnesses told police that a group of strangers had invited Maricle to join them for drinks, after which he was not seen again. On April 8, 2003, authorities found Maricle's decomposed body in rural Monterey County, buried in a plastic drum. The corpse, bearing signs of torture, was identified from dental records.

Five days later, police arrested three suspects in Maricle's kidnapping, torture, and murder. Prosecutors identified the suspects—Dominique England, Daymon Schrock, and Jeanne Soja—as members of a well-known prison gang, the Nazi Low Riders. Prosecutors described Maricle's murder as a hate crime, motivated by the fact that he was bisexual. All three defendants pled guilty to murder and kidnapping in May 2003.

## STGS

Prison officials describe gangs as Security Threat Groups, or STGs, because they disrupt prison discipline with violence, bribery, and smuggling of contraband. STGs operate along the same lines as other gangs, with chapters in various prisons, but their history reverses that of "normal" gangs. Instead of starting on the street and being sent to prison, these gangsters organize in prison, then extend their criminal influence back into the "free world" through their visitors and members on parole.

Most prison gangs begin as self-defense organizations, protecting their members from attack by enemies. A few start when established gangs suffer a split between two would-be leaders. Most prison gangs restrict their membership by race, with some adding religious or political requirements for prospective members.

In prison, STGs behave much as gangs on the street, fighting for turf, dealing in contraband and prostitution, loan-sharking, and bribing authorities. Outside of prison, members pursue the same activities, along with kidnapping, illegal arms deals, and contract murders. For many gangs, a pledge of "blood in, blood out" dictates that new recruits must kill to gain full membership, and they are bound to serve the gang until they die.

## LA EME

America's first recognized prison gang was the Mexican Mafia, also known as *La Eme* ("M" in Spanish). It was organized in 1957 at a juvenile prison in Tracy, California. Its founders were *sureños*, Hispanic gang members from southern California, who ranked among the first gang members to use colored bandanas as a gang symbol. Many members also wear tattoos including the number 13 (for *M*, the alphabet's 13th letter).

Authorities rank *La Eme* as America's most active STG, with 30,000 members nationwide. The gang's primary activity is drug trafficking, though some chapters are satisfied to "tax" smugglers without handling the drugs themselves. Discipline within the gang is brutal, including murder of gay members.

Ironically, despite *La Eme*'s emphasis on racial solidarity, it sometimes collaborates with the racist Aryan Brotherhood against another Hispanic gang, *Nuestra Familia*. Members also fight with African-American inmates.

Recent criminal cases involving *La Eme* include the May 1997 conviction of 12 members on federal racketeering charges that resulted in life sentences; the February 2001 conviction of member Mariano Martinez on 24 felony charges, including three counts of murder; and the August 2004 federal drug-trafficking indictment of 26 members in Texas. Four defendants in that case pled guilty during 2006.

## BLACK GUERRILLA FAMILY

California inmate George Jackson (see sidebar) founded America's first political prison gang in 1966 at San Quentin prison. Jackson recruited members for his Black Guerrilla Family (BGF), or Black Vanguard, with lessons on Marxist economics and black liberation.

The BGF accepts members from various ghetto street gangs as long as they accept the group's political message and stop

## ♀ SOLEDAD BROTHER

George Lester Jackson (1941–71) founded the Black Guerrilla Family in 1966 while serving time at California's San Quentin prison for a $70 holdup that he committed at age 18. In January 1970, authorities accused Jackson and two other inmates of killing a white guard. Instead of facing trial for murder, they were placed in solitary confinement at Soledad prison.

There, Jackson joined the Black Panther Party and penned many letters supporting black liberation. Those letters were later published in book form as *Soledad Brother* (1970) and *Blood in My Eye* (1972), making Jackson a national celebrity.

In August 1970 Jackson's younger brother tried to free three San Quentin inmates from the Marin County courthouse, sparking a shootout that left four persons dead (including a judge) and several more badly wounded. FBI agents charged black activist Angela Davis with providing guns for the breakout, but jurors found her not guilty.

A year later, on August 21, 1971, lawyer Stephen Bingham visited Jackson in prison. Guards searched Jackson before the visit, but later claimed that he returned to his cellblock with a pistol hidden underneath an Afro wig. In the resultant battle, six persons died, including Jackson, three guards, and two white prisoners.

Authorities charged Bingham with smuggling the gun to Jackson. Bingham dodged police for 13 years, then surrendered for trial in 1984. Jurors acquitted him of all charges, leaving many unanswered questions about George Jackson's death. Police informant Louis Tackwood later claimed that law enforcement officers paid him to plan Jackson's murder in prison. Another theory blames Black Panther leaders who were jealous of Jackson's role in the party.

fighting among themselves. Members also cooperate with *Nuestra Familia* against the Mexican Mafia and Aryan Brotherhood. Free world allies of the BGF have included the Black Liberation Army, the mostly white Weather Underground group, and the Symbionese Liberation Army (which kidnapped heiress Patty Hearst in 1974).

While the BGF's political stance opposes drug dealing and most other mercenary crimes, prison officials regard the group as highly dangerous to guards and inmates it has marked as enemies. The BGF's constitution specifies death for members who use heroin or furnish weapons to the gang's enemies. In 1987, the BGF rejected an alliance to kill prison guards, proposed by the Aryan Brotherhood.

## ARYAN BROTHERHOOD

This white racist gang was organized at San Quentin in 1967, as a white response to the Black Guerrilla Family. Its members espouse the Nazi "master race" theories of Adolf Hitler (1889–1945) and display tattoos with racist themes proclaiming their supposed "100% pure" bloodlines. Unlike the BGF, however, the Aryan Brotherhood's (AB) politics do not prevent members from participation in drug deals, prostitution, and other crimes. Many members also belong to outlaw motorcycle gangs (see Chapter 4).

Prison allies of the Brotherhood include the Nazi Low Riders and (strangely) the Mexican Mafia. Bitter opponents include *Nuestra Familia,* the BGF, and other nonwhite inmates. Free world allies include racist groups such as the Aryan Nations and the Ku Klux Klan.

Despite its racism, the AB sometimes uses African-American inmates to smuggle drugs and perform other low-level tasks. It also lends "moral support" to black convicts when they disrupt the system, and once proposed an alliance with the BGF to kill prison guards. In the 1980s, although AB members made up only 1 percent of California's prison population, they committed 24 percent of the state's prison assaults and murders. The three racists who fatally tortured black hitchhiker James Byrd Jr. at Jasper, Texas, in June 1998, wore tattoos suggesting affiliation with the Aryan Brotherhood.

## NUESTRA FAMILIA

*Nuestra Familia* ("our family," in Spanish) was founded in 1967 by Hispanic inmates at California's Soledad prison. Unlike the Mexican Mafia, its members are *norteños*, from northern California, a geographic rivalry that outweighs racial solidarity. The gangs are bitter enemies, with members of *Nuestra Familia* sporting red bandanas (versus *La Eme*'s blue) and tattoos including the number 14 (for *N*, the alphabet's 14th letter).

Those differences aside, it is difficult to tell the rival gangs apart. Both limit membership to Mexican-American inmates, proclaim themselves defenders of *La Raza* (the Hispanic race), and participate in widespread drug trafficking. Like other prison gangsters, members of *Nuestra Familia* obey a written list of "household policies" or suffer punishment.

While *Nuestra Familia* was founded to protect *norteño* inmates from *sureño* enemies, its list of rivals soon expanded to include the Aryan Brotherhood and other racist gangs. Allies include the BGF and a spin-off gang, the Northern Structure, which some observers believe was created by *Nuestra Familia* leaders as a diversion.

State and federal authorities have cooperated to disrupt *Nuestra Familia* in recent years. Throughout 2000, federal prosecutors indicted 22 members on racketeering charges. Thirteen pled guilty in 2001, followed by five acknowledged leaders in September 2005. In January 2006, California governor Arnold Schwarzenegger canceled their state prison terms so that they could be scattered in federal prisons across the country.

## NETA

Neta is another political STG, created in 1970 by inmates at Puerto Rico's Rio Pedras prison. Its members support Puerto Rican nationalism, seeking independence from the United States (although the gang's colors are red, white, and blue). Neta recruits Puerto Rican inmates in prisons across the country.

While rated dangerous to prison staff and other convicts, Neta members keep a low profile, letting *Nuestra Familia* and *La Eme* take the bad publicity. Gang allies in the free world include *Los Macheteros*, a violent group of Puerto Rican revolutionaries. Rival gangs include the Latin Kings and *Los Solidos*. Members are noted for their hatred of police and do not hesitate to kill if threatened with arrest.

## TEXAS SYNDICATE

Another Latino gang, the Texas Syndicate, was organized in 1974 by Texas felons serving time at California's Folsom Prison. Upon release, the founders returned to Texas and were later jailed there, creating new chapters. Members include natives of Mexico, Colombia, and Cuba. Despite the gang's philosophy of Hispanic supremacy, it constantly feuds with both the Mexican Mafia and

Members of the Texas Syndicate prison gang show off their tattoos.
Andrew Lichtenstein/Corbis

*Nuestra Familia,* while forging alliances with Caucasian gangs like the Dirty White Boys. Recruits wear "TS" tattoos on various parts of their bodies.

## CRIPS VS. BLOODS

It was only a matter of time before America's two largest ghetto street gangs, the Crips and Bloods (see Chapter 6), created spin-off prison gangs. California inmates founded the Consolidated Crip Organization in 1985, followed by creation of the United Blood Nation (UBN), or Red Rags, two years later. Curiously, the UBN got its start at Rikers Island, a lockup in New York City, where black inmates organized in self-defense against the rival Latin Kings. Some observers claim that the UBN simply imitates members of the west coast Bloods, while others believe the two groups are closely linked.

One major project of the Consolidated Crip Organization is maintenance of peace between inmates from different Crip factions, who frequently kill each other outside of prison. No such truce is recognized with the United Blood Nation. Both groups deal drugs and take time off from their feuding to battle with Hispanic and white-racist gangs.

## NAZI LOW RIDERS

America's newest significant STG, the Nazi Low Riders (NLR), was organized at California's Pelican Bay prison in 1992. Founders included members of the Aryan Brotherhood and another white gang, the Peckerwoods, who were confined as habitual troublemakers at Pelican Bay's Security Housing Unit. Despite that racist background, the NLR also accepts a few light-skinned Hispanics as members. By 1998, the gang had an estimated 1,300 members.

Unlike the other STGs examined here, the NLR admits both male and female members, all of whom are expected to serve as drug couriers and contract killers. Acts linked to the NLR in southern California include a mixture of drug-related offenses and random attacks on African Americans. NLR members also have a history of violent assaults against police officers.

## "BLOOD IN, BLOOD OUT"

The standard STG code guarantees that prison gang members are often involved in violent incidents, including murders and severe assaults. Victims include members of rival gangs, police and prison staff, and STG members subject to brutal discipline from their own leaders.

Law enforcement statistics tell the grim story. Between 1975 and 1985, Aryan Brotherhood members committed 40 murders in California prisons, plus 13 more in free world communities. In federal prisons, AB members killed 26 victims (including three guards) between 1978 and 1992. Nationwide, American prisons suffered 96 gang-related murders in 1977 alone. Texas prisons recorded 52 gang murders during 1984–86. Recent years have seen violent prison disturbances in general on the rise.

Official spokesmen reported 15 STGs active in federal prisons across the United States during 1990. Two years later, they declared that prison gangs were dying out, but that announcement was premature. In 1994, Florida alone claimed 240 active prison gangs. Two years later, the total was 260 and rising, with no end in sight.

## GANG RECRUITMENT AND SUPPRESSION

While some convicts enter prison as gang members, other inmates join gangs for various reasons. Foremost among those is protection from members of other races or ethnic groups in an environment where whites, blacks, Asians, and Hispanics are constantly involved in hostile racist action. Thus, while same-race members of different gangs might fight each other, racially integrated prison gangs are virtually nonexistent.

Some gang members enlist voluntarily, as a matter of personal belief or racial prejudice, while others are coerced by fellow inmates to join a particular gang. Coerced recruitment may involve inmates with special skills (legal training, computer skills, etc.), or may be used more broadly if a gang simply wants to increase its mass membership. Inmates who refuse to join a gang upon demand often find themselves under attack by all sides.

Prison administrators use various means to control gang activity. Minor offenses are generally punished with loss of various privileges, while some hard-core gang members spend most of their time

The ADX Supermax Prison in Florence, Colorado, is a state-of-the-art isolation prison for repeat and high-profile felony offenders. *Lizzie Himmel/Sygma/Corbis*

in tightly controlled "administrative segregation." Since the 1990s, special control unit prisons—also called Administrative Maximum (ADX) prisons—have been established for gang members and other high-risk inmates throughout the United States. In the federal ADX prison at Terre Haute, Indiana, prisoners spend at least 22 hours per day in solitary confinement.

# Crips and Bloods

Between 1940 and 1944, the African American population of Los Angeles increased 100 percent, prompting white racists to lash out violently at blacks. Hate groups like the Ku Klux Klan resurfaced, while gangs like the Spook Hunters attacked black youths on sight. Soon, defensive gangs formed in the ghettos of Compton, Watts, and South Central L.A. Despite constant fighting over the next 15 years, deaths were rare. Police recorded only six gang murders during 1960.

The Watts riot of 1965 sparked new militancy among ghetto gangs in Los Angeles, encouraged by social and political groups like the Black Muslims and the Black Panther Party. Law enforcement targeted those groups, but largely ignored street gangs until 1969, when a new force appeared on the L.A. scene.

## CRIPPIN'

Raymond "Truck" Washington was only 15 in 1969 when he founded the Baby Avenues, also known as the Avenue Cribs. The name was later changed to Crips, either because some early members fought with canes (and were nicknamed "cripples") or because the slang term "crippin'" referred to criminal activity. In 1971, Stanley "Tookie" Williams formed the West Side Crips, while Washington ran the East Side crew. Crips committed their first known murder in February 1972, killing a 53-year-old man for his leather jacket.

The Crips expanded rapidly. By 1972, eight gangs used the name in Los Angeles County. That number increased to 45 in 1978, 109 in 1982, and 199 by the early 1990s. Meanwhile, Crip factions sprang up across the United States and in other parts of the world. Belize, in Central America, had its own Crips by 1989, when members migrated to eight U.S. states.

Expansion of the Crips brought trouble from within. Feuds broke out between different Crip sets (neighborhood gangs), and soon the "brothers" were busily killing each other. Ambushes and drive-by shootings multiplied. Founder Ray Washington was gunned down in 1979, at age 26.

## SLOBS VS. CRABS

When not killing one another, Crips preyed on other gangs, expanding their turf. In 1972, leaders of various non-Crip gangs, including the L.A. Brims and the Piru Street Boys, united to resist Crip attacks. They called themselves Bloods, adopting red bandanas since the Crips wore blue. Crips called their new rivals *slobs*, while Bloods referred to Crips as *crabs*. The British Knights athletic shoes favored by Crips were nicknamed "Blood Killas." Bloods dropped the letter "C" from their names, or added a "K" afterward, to mean "Crip Killer."

With such hatred between them, violence was inevitable. Los Angeles witnessed 70 gang-related murders in 1974, increasing to 355 in 1980 and 803 in 1992. During the same period, ghetto youths created 295 new gangs. An estimated 13,500 gang members inhabited L.A., outnumbered only by New York City's 24,000. According to the Department of Justice's 2005 National Gang Threat Assessment, there are at least 21,500 gangs in the United States, with more than 731,000 active members.

Like the Crips, Bloods soon expanded into other states across America. As members of both gangs were sent to prison, they reorganized inside the walls, forming the rival Consolidated Crip Organization and the United Blood Nation. Both groups sought peace within their separate gangs, without much success. Meanwhile, a founder of the Crips was fighting for his life.

## TOOKIE

Stanley "Tookie" Williams (1953–2005) claimed that he joined the Crips at age 18 to help suppress street gangs. His logic was fuzzy, and he did not succeed. Instead, he murdered four victims during two robberies in early 1979. Firearms experts linked shotgun shells found at the crime scenes to a gun owned by Williams. Jurors convicted him in 1981 and he received a death sentence.

In prison, Williams remained an active member of the Crips. Between 1981 and 1993, he spent six and one-half years in solitary confinement for attacking guards and other inmates. In 1994 he seemed to change, renouncing gangs, apologizing for his role in the Crips, and writing several anti-gang books for children. In 2005 Williams published a memoir, *Blue Rage, Black Redemption.*

The change impressed many people. Friends nominated Williams for the Nobel Peace Prize five times (2001–05). In 2004 Oscar-winner Jamie Foxx portrayed Williams in *Redemption,* a made-for-TV movie. President George W. Bush sent Williams a commendation for his social activism. None of it would save his life, however. His appeals ran out on December 13, 2005, when Williams was executed by lethal injection.

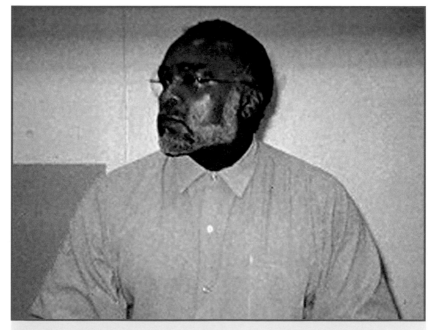

This April 2000 photo shows Stanley "Tookie" Williams, founder of the West Side Crips. *California Department of Corrections/Handout/ Reuters/Corbis*

## CRACK ATTACK

Tookie Williams went to jail before the Crips and Bloods entered their most violent phase, sparked by the 1980s invention of crack or rock cocaine. Crack is highly addictive and simple to make, a combination that quickly made it the poor addict's favorite drug. For gangsters who made and sold it, crack was the greatest bonanza since Congress banned liquor in 1920. More violence followed. In Los Angeles alone, gang-related murders increased 226 percent between 1980 and 1992.

Gangland slayings aside, politicians treated crack as a deadly plague. New federal laws made crack the only drug for which simple possession of five grams triggers a mandatory five-year minimum jail term. In fact, first-time crack offenders in federal court commonly receive prison terms of 10 and a half years. Possessing five grams of any other drug—including powder cocaine—remains a misdemeanor, punishable by one year or less in prison. Some critics charge that the harsh crack penalties discriminate against poor addicts and people of color.

But in any case, the zero-tolerance program does not seem to work. During 2000–01, DEA agents arrested 11,675 persons for crack possession, while local police jailed thousands more. Seventeen percent of men and 25 percent of women arrested for all crimes nationwide in 2003 admitted using crack. In 2005, an average 3 percent of American students in grades eight through 12 admitted "lifetime use" of crack cocaine.

## TRUCE? WHAT TRUCE?

In 1992 another violent spasm gripped Los Angeles. Police were caught on videotape, beating black motorist Rodney King after a high-speed car chase. White jurors acquitted the officers of assault on April 29, 1992. A three-day ghetto riot that left 40 persons dead, 2,000 injured, and 8,000 in jail followed in protest against the verdict.

Crips and Bloods responded to that outbreak by announcing a truce between their gangs. They also proposed a dramatic face-lift for L.A., including street repairs, new landscaping and lighting, construction of new parks health facilities, low-interest loans to ghetto businesses, tighter supervision of police, and $500 million worth of improvements for inner-city schools.

In return for that massive investment, gang leaders said they would match government spending on AIDS research and "encourage" L.A. drug lords to stop selling crack. Skeptics noted that Crips and Bloods were the drug lords, suggesting that their truce simply allowed the gangs to spend more time on profitable crimes. The truce resulted in a temporary cessation of violence between Crips and Bloods, while violence between rival Crip sets, between larger gangs and their smaller competitors, and with other gangs continued.

Civic leaders in L.A. later complained that the truce was "flimsy" and short-lived. By 2002, the city boasted 150,000 gang members in 1,300 sets. Gangs were blamed for 51 percent of all local murders that year, claiming 587 lives.

Two years after the supposed truce in Los Angeles, leading Crips and Bloods in Fort Worth, Texas, announced a similar ceasefire. Chiefs of six gang factions announced the treaty on television on February 25, 1994. Police noted that Fort Worth harbored some 3,900 gang members, responsible for 173 drive-by shootings (with 16 deaths) in 1993 alone.

Another decade passed before the next announcement of a truce between the Crips and Bloods in May 2004. This time the word came from Newark, New Jersey, where gangsters had killed 46 victims in four months. Reporters credited Tookie Williams for drafting the peace plan, but police had little hope that it would succeed.

## MUSIC TO DIE FOR

Turf and crack are not the only friction points between the Crips and Bloods. From the early 1990s onward, music in the form of gangsta rap or hip-hop also provided more fuel for violence between feuding gangs.

Gangsta rap, with its lyrics emphasizing weapons, crime, and abuse of women, was alarming enough on its own to some critics. Concern only deepened when performers such as Snoop Dogg, Daz Dillinger, Tray Deee, Kurupt, Eazy-E, MC Ren, Nate Dogg, Warren G, and Tone Lōc advertised their association with various Crip factions. At the same time, a popular hip-hop dance called the "Crip-walk," or "C-walk," was interpreted by many as a calculated insult to the Bloods.

# 🎙 RAP WARS

In the mid-1990s, a feud between gangsta rappers in New York and California climaxed with the violent deaths of two popular hip-hop stars. Tupac Shakur (1971–96) and Christopher "Notorious B.I.G." Wallace (1972–97) were both born in New York, but Shakur later moved to Los Angeles. Stories differ on the source of his quarrel with Wallace, but the men were enemies by 1996, insulting one another in their lyrics and in public comments.

On September 7, 1996, Shakur and Knight attended a boxing match in Las Vegas. After the fight, they beat up a Crip who earlier had attacked one of Shakur's bodyguards. At 11:14 p.m., unknown gunmen ambushed Knight's car, fatally wounding Shakur. He died at a local hospital six days later. Yafeu Fula, a friend of Shakur who witnessed the slaying and said he could identify the gunman, was killed in New Jersey soon after the Las Vegas shooting.

Six years later, *Los Angeles Times* reporter Chuck Phillips quoted unnamed Crips members accusing Christopher Wallace of plotting Shakur's death. According to that story, B.I.G. used Crips as bodyguards and put a $1 million contract on Shakur's life, even providing a gun for the murder. Unfortunately, when that story was published in 2002, Wallace could not respond.

By then, he was already dead.

On March 9, 1997, Wallace attended a party sponsored by *VIBE* magazine in Los Angeles. Afterward, while his car was stopped at a red light, drive-by shooters hit him with six bullets, killing him instantly. Wallace's death, like Shakur's, remains officially unsolved.

Some friends of Wallace blamed Suge Knight and his Blood allies for the murder, one of several killings linked to Knight in accusations that never produced any criminal charges. Knight *has* been imprisoned on weapons charges and for parole violations, while performers including Snoop Dogg and Vanilla Ice accuse him of misusing their money for personal gain. In February 2005 he was jailed on drug charges. Six months later, Knight was wounded

Christopher Wallace, AKA The Notorious B.I.G., is escorted to a police car in New York in March 1996. Wallace's March 1997 death remains unsolved. *AP Photo/Adam Nadel*

in a Florida shooting incident. Lawsuits drove Death Row Records into bankruptcy in April 2006.

On March 17, 2005, jurors convicted rapper Kimberly "Lil' Kim" Jones of conspiracy and perjury for lying to a Manhattan grand jury about her friends' involvement in a 2001 shooting incident. Jones and her entourage were leaving the Hot 97 studios in New York City when they met rival musicians Foxy Brown and friends of the rap duo Capone-N-Noreaga. Under oath, Jones denied that her manager and another friend were at the scene, but video surveillance cameras caught them on tape. Jones received a 366-day prison sentence, later reporting that she wrote 200 songs while incarcerated.

Controversy still surrounds the C-walk, pioneered by rapper Ice-T in the late 1980s. Despite its later mainstream popularity, Snoop Dogg declared (in lyrics of his song "Drop It Like It's Hot") that the jerky steps were meant for Crips gang members only. MTV censored the steps from Snoop's video of "Drop It," but the same moves later appeared in videos by Jesse Dasilva, Korn, Westside Connection, and Xzibit, as well as in the movie *You Got Served* (2004).

Crips are not alone in their affinity for gangsta rap. Marion "Suge" Knight, founder of Death Row Records, allegedly maintains links to the Bloods. Hip-hop performers known for admitted ties to the Bloods include rapper/producer DJ Quick, Jayceon "The Game" Taylor, and the group Damu Ridaz. Critics claim that gang-allied performers use their music to threaten rivals and to celebrate when they are killed or wounded.

# New World Disorder

By the 1980s, American history had come full circle. New waves of immigration brought thousands of strangers to the United States, putting new strain on the great melting pot. As in the nineteenth century, some new arrivals had been felons in their homelands. Others drifted into gangs for self-defense or tracked the scent of easy money into criminal careers. And once again, as during Prohibition in the 1920s, the chaotic war on drugs gave gangs a shot at wealth beyond their wildest dreams.

## EAST MEETS WEST

Asian crime syndicates have operated in America for many years. Chinese Tongs (or Triads) gained a foothold in the nineteenth century, while the Japanese *Yakuza* arrived after World War II. Both groups participate in the narcotics trade, illegal gambling, and other crimes, while "laundering" billions of dollars through legal investments.

At the same time, Chinese street gangs have wreaked havoc in their own communities, from coast to coast. The most notorious include

- *Wah Ching,* founded in San Francisco's Chinatown during the 1960s by Cantonese youths from Hong Kong. In 1977 a shoot-out with the rival *Chung Ching Yee* (Joe Boys) left five persons dead and 11 wounded at the Golden Dragon Restaurant.

Dissension later split the gang; driven out by rivals, it relocated in Los Angeles. In 2001, a 17-year-old member shot and killed two members of the San Gabriel Killas at a high school football game. In December 2005, another *Wah Ching* gangster killed a Latino man by repeatedly driving over him with a car.

- Ghost Shadows, a gang that dominated New York City's Chinatown from the mid-1970s through the early 1990s. Members engaged in drug trafficking, gambling, robbery, and extortion. Many "ABC" (American-born Chinese) businessmen supported the Ghost Shadows in controlling new "FOB" (fresh off the boat) immigrants. Ghost Shadows terrorized members of rival gangs, driving the competition out of business by 1985, when federal prosecutors charged 25 members with 85 crimes, including 13 murders. All were convicted and sentenced to prison.
- United Bamboo, founded on Taiwan in 1957 and later transplanted to America by immigrants who focus mainly on gambling for income. The gang stresses harmony and "good social connections," but resorts to violence if challenged by rivals.

America's withdrawal from Vietnam in 1972–75 prompted a flood of refugees from communism to the United States, including certain criminal elements. Some Vietnamese hoodlums joined Chinese street gangs, while others formed their own groups specializing in robbery, auto theft, and extortion. Southern California is the heart of Vietnamese gang activity, but various groups are found nationwide. Prominent groups include

- Born to Kill (BTK), New York's most notorious Vietnamese gang during the late 1980s and early 1990s. In July 1990, a shootout at the funeral of a BTK member in Linden, New Jersey, left seven persons injured. Gang founder David Thai and several others received life prison terms without parole in October 1992 on charges that included murder, robbery, extortion, ransom kidnapping, and other violent crimes. In court, Thai also admitted earning more than $13 million from sales of counterfeit Rolex watches.
- West Philly Woo Boys, active in Philadelphia around the University of Pennsylvania campus, where its members steal cars, operate "protection" rackets, and stage home-invasion robberies. Police estimate the gang has 20–25 hard-core members.

- Asian Boyz, active in Long Beach, California, since the 1980s. Members range in age from 12 to 40 and commit a wide variety of crimes. In the 1990s, videotapes of a pool hall shootout between Asian Boyz and the Tiny Raskal gang were broadcast on *America's Most Wanted,* leading to the arrests of several suspects.
- Oriental Troops, founded in Visalia, California, in 1996, including members from Laos and Thailand. Originally formed in self-defense against attacks by Latino gangs, this group has expanded to Seattle, Washington. Members sell drugs imported from Mexico.
- Masters of Destruction (MOD), organized in Fresno, California, by members of Vietnam's Hmong minority. As during wartime, the Hmongs are tenacious fighters. Their modern rivals include the Crips and other Asian gangs. The MOD has chapters nationwide, with special strength reported in Colorado, Minnesota, and Wisconsin. Its female branch is the Ladies of Destruction.
- Oriental Ruthless Boyz, another Hmong gang, founded in Long Beach, California. It later spread to challenge the Masters of Destruction in Fresno. Other known enemies include the Crips, White Tigers, and Mongolian Boys.

## BOAT PEOPLE

Between April and October 1980, Cuban dictator Fidel Castro opened Mariel Harbor for a mass exodus of refugees to the United States. An estimated 125,000 Cubans fled to America aboard 1,700 boats of all sizes, most landing in Florida. Immigration officials soon discovered that some were criminals and mental patients, deported from Cuban prisons and psychiatric hospitals.

After detention in various camps throughout the United States, some *Marielitos,* as these refugees were sometimes called, joined gangs or created their own in cities from Miami to Las Vegas and Los Angeles. Their crimes included robbery and drug trafficking, often in league with Colombian cocaine syndicates. Films about the Mariel boatlift and its violent aftermath include *Scarface* (1983) and *Before Night Falls* (2000).

Another Caribbean source of "boat people" is Haiti. Around the time of the Mariel boatlift, 25,000 Haitians also landed in Florida. The U.S. Coast Guard intercepted another 109,496 Haitian refugees

A shrimp boat returning from Cuba is packed with Cuban refugees as it lands at Florida's Key West Naval Base in April 1980. *AP Photo*

between 1982 and early 2006. In Miami, where many remain, police identify 40 Haitian-American gangs. An example of their violence is the machine-gun ambush that killed three men and wounded another on June 5, 2006. In May 2006, another drive-by shooting killed two bystanders, one of them a toddler.

## JAMAICAN POSSES

Jamaican gangs, known as "posses," appeared in America during the early 1980s. Their main commodities were guns and marijuana, but some factions began selling crack cocaine in 1986. That change sparked warfare between followers of the Rastafarian religion (which opposes hard drugs) and others who ignore the sect's teachings.

Most posses in America belong to one of two broad coalitions: the Shower Posse (allied with the Jamaican Labor Party) or the Spangler Posse (linked to the People's National Party). During Jamaica's 1980 elections, posse members killed an estimated 500 victims in political disputes. In America, the Justice Department blames posse gunmen for more than 1,400 murders between 1985 and 1997. In 1988, after a series of drug raids in 14 states, federal agents estimated that posses controlled 40 percent of the nation's crack traffic.

Jamaican gangsters are known for their extreme violence, including ritual execution of enemies that requires four shots to the chest and one to the head. Some sources claim the Shower Posse earned its name by showering its enemies with bullets in public places.

## FILIPINO GANGS

The United States owned the Philippines from 1898 to 1946 and many natives of that island nation live in the United States today. As with any other group, some turn to crime. Known Filipino gangs include

- *Satanas*, the oldest group in Los Angeles, organized for self-defense from other gangs in the 1960s. Within a decade, members proved their willingness to kill and prospered in the drug trade. Alliances come and go, making various Hispanic gangsters friends one day and enemies the next. Since the 1980s, *Satanas* has expanded throughout California, with chapters in Washington, Canada, and Mexico.
- *Samahang Dugong Pinoy*, founded in Los Angeles during the 1990s. The gang soon spread into neighboring cities and states as concerned parents tried to move their sons away from trouble. Typical crimes range from shoplifting and underage drinking to drive-by shootings. Rivals include the Crips and Asian Boyz.
- The Vargas Family, also known as the Filipino Mafia, tattoos its members with the numeral "6" (for the number of letters in "Vargas"). Members coexist peacefully with most black and Hispanic gangs, but feud constantly with the spin-off Ramirez gang.

- *Sarzana*, launched by Filipino immigrants in Los Angeles during the late 1980s. The group later opened its ranks to natives of Korea and other Asian countries, becoming one of America's few multiracial gangs.

## COMRADES IN ARMS

The collapse of communist regimes in Eastern Europe and Russia (1989–91) created new opportunities for immigration and gang-related crime. The so-called Russian Mafia, including some 100,000 members of 8,000 different gangs, today controls an estimated 75 percent of all private business and 40 percent of all wealth in the former Soviet Union. Moscow police investigated more than 5,000 murders and 20,000 other violent crimes in 1993 alone—many of them gang related. Foreign businesses in Russia pay gangsters 20 percent of their profits each year for "protection."

With so much cash on hand, gang members from Russia and other ex-communist states travel widely throughout the world, dealing in weapons, drugs, and prostitution. New York's Brighton Beach is known as a hotbed of Russian criminal activity, but members of various gangs can be found nationwide.

By 1997, police estimated that 80 percent of all professional hockey players in Russia were making protection payments to Russian gangsters, under threat of injury or death. Other crimes favored by Russian gangs include insurance fraud and long-distance bank robbery using computers to transfer funds.

In New York's borough of the Bronx, police report trouble from a new gang called Albanian Boys Incorporated. Its members are the sons of immigrants from Albania and other Balkan nations, including 5,000 refugees from the 1990s "ethnic cleansing" in Serbia. As with many other gangs before it, the Albanian Boys first organized for self-defense, then expanded into criminal pursuits.

## OUT OF AFRICA

No continent is free of gangs, and Africa has suffered more than its share of violence from tyrants and warlords in recent years. While much of the bloodshed arises from politics, religion, and tribal hatred, Nigerian gangsters devote themselves to smuggling drugs and killing those who try to interfere.

Drug traffic from Nigeria was so extensive by 1993 that U.S. leaders canceled all direct flights from that country to America.

## ♀ HATE ON TRIAL

On November 13, 1988, members of a skinhead gang called East Side White Pride attacked Ethiopian student Mulugeta Seraw in Portland, Oregon, beating him to death with baseball bats. A member of the gang, jailed on unrelated charges four days later, identified the killers for police. Ringleader Kenneth Mieske pled guilty to murder in 1989, receiving a prison term of 30 years to life. Two others pled guilty to manslaughter and received 20-year terms.

Meanwhile, leaders of the Southern Poverty Law Center (SPLC) discovered that East Side White Pride was linked to a larger hate group, White Aryan Resistance (WAR). Thomas Metzger founded WAR in 1983 after resigning from the California Ku Klux Klan. With his son John, Metzger recruited Nazi skinheads across the country, calling for violence against Jews and nonwhites. SPLC investigators learned that WAR members had furnished East Side White Pride with hate literature and the baseball bats used to kill Mulugeta Seraw.

On November 27, 1989, Seraw's family and the SPLC sued WAR, the Metzgers, and Seraw's killers for wrongful death. At trial, a year later, WAR member Dave Mazzella told jurors that Tom and John Metzger instructed skinheads to attack racial minorities. Another WAR witness admitted teaching skinheads "how to break bones and crush skulls." On October 22, 1990, jurors ordered the defendants to pay $12.5 million in damages.

That verdict forced the Metzgers and WAR into bankruptcy, but it did not silence their voices of hatred. In 1991, Tom Metzger received a six-month jail term and 300 hours of community service for cross burning (a form of racist intimidation). A year later, both Metzgers were charged with violating court orders that barred them from traveling to Canada. Today, they advocate "lone wolf" attacks against minorities and the American government.[1]

The State Department also decertified Nigeria, which identifies the nation as not fully cooperative with the United States in the effort to control illegal drugs and renders it ineligible for U.S. economic aid. Those measures made life harder for Nigeria's poor residents and would-be immigrants, but they failed to block drug smuggling, and direct flights resumed in 1999.

American authorities describe a "chain of drug barons" controlling narcotics traffic from Nigeria. Ten alleged leaders were jailed in 1994, followed by 27 more a year later, but the trade still thrives. Nigerian firing squads executed drug dealers until 1984, when public protest stopped the practice. Neither death nor any other threatened punishment has so far stemmed the tide.

Skinheads saluting in a march against the Martin Luther King holiday.
Mark Peterson/Corbis

## RAHOWA!

As with the "British invasion" of musicians and artists in the 1960s, skinhead styles bridged the Atlantic from England to the United States in the mid-1980s. While skinheads (like all people) adopt various political beliefs, the most notorious are neo-Nazi thugs who hate minorities and claim RAHOWA (for *racial holy war*) as their fighting slogan.

By 1990 America harbored some 3,000 hard-core skinheads, dispersed among 95 gangs in 34 states. Between 1986 and 1989, they were responsible for at least six murders and 52 assaults, plus countless threats and acts of vandalism. Skinhead numbers have declined in the twenty-first century, but a survey conducted in early 2006 found 56 gangs active in 24 states.

Male skinheads (and some females) commonly shave their heads, sport Nazi or Viking tattoos, and engage in drunken assaults on Jews, nonwhites, and gays. Nationwide, many gangs are linked to adult racist groups such as the Aryan Nations, the Ku Klux Klan, and White Aryan Resistance. They often join in public demonstrations by those groups, sometimes assaulting police or bystanders. Group stompings—known as boot parties—are a common skinhead practice.

Typical skinhead gangs active in Spring 2006 included the Brotherhood of the Chosen, the Connecticut White Wolves, the Retaliator Skinhead Nation, the White Power Liberation Front, and the TCB Hate Crew (short for *taking care of business*). Many modern skinheads subscribe to the tenets of Christian Identity, which teaches that Jews are the physical children of Satan and nonwhite "mud people" evolved from crossbreeding between humans and apes.

# Gangs in
# Fiction and Film

Americans are fascinated by gangs and gangsters. People may not cheer and chase them through the streets as if they were movie stars or musicians, but the public still derives a thrill from their outlandish criminal adventures. True-crime books have been best sellers in America since Jesse James launched his career in robbery after the Civil War.

But people want more.

The public is not satisfied with media reports of real-life crimes, no matter how bizarre. They want more action, more flamboyant criminals with catchy nicknames, more explosive brawls and shootouts.

For some, the tales are pure excitement, thrill rides stripped of any risk, with happy endings that are rare in daily life. Others believe that they can learn something from fictional portrayals of the gangster's world—perhaps a way to end such criminal enterprises in the near future.

## THE PRINTED PAGE

Gang-oriented novels are often published for young readers and assigned in schools. The thoughtful works of author S. E. Hinton, including *The Outsiders* (1967), *That Was Then, This Is Now* (1971), and *Rumble Fish* (1975), are familiar in American classrooms. All explore the lives of troubled youths who are driven into gang-related danger by the kinds of family problems many teenagers face every day.

Other novels about gangland life include Harlan Ellison's *Rumble* (1958), Frank Bonham's *Durango Street* (1965), Sol Yurick's *The Warriors* (1965), Sharon Draper's *Romiette and Julio* (1999), Walter Myers's *Scorpions* (1988), and Richard Wright's *Rite of Passage* (1994).

Each provides a different view of gang life, without glamorizing the violent world of crime.

## HOLLYWOOD'S WILD WEST

Frontier outlaw gangs inspired countless dime novels in the nineteenth century, and they remain popular subjects for Hollywood filmmakers. Trail dust and gun smoke have excited movie fans for nearly 100 years, with no end in sight.

New Mexico outlaw William "Billy the Kid" Bonney leads the list of Hollywood anti-heroes, with 31 movies since 1911. The James-Younger gang, despite its greater fame in life, trails Billy with 21 films spanning 80 years.

The Dalton gang has rated three films. Butch Cassidy's Hole-in-the-Wall gang inspired two classic films in 1969, *The Wild Bunch* and *Butch Cassidy and the Sundance Kid*.

While Westerns periodically go in and out of style in Hollywood, it seems safe to say that we have not seen the last of America's frontier outlaws on movie or television screens.

## PUBLIC ENEMIES

Like the Wild West, America's lawless years of 1920–36 have inspired dozens of movies depicting famous public enemies. Most of the films broadcast the lesson that "crime doesn't pay"—a message sometimes contradicted by the lavish lifestyle of actual gangsters.

Prohibition-era bootleggers appear, sometimes thinly disguised with fictitious names.

John Dillinger, Charles "Pretty Boy" Floyd, George "Baby Face" Nelson, "Machine Gun" Kelly, and "Ma" Barker have also featured in multiple Hollywood films.

Robert Redford (left) as the Sundance Kid and Paul Newman as Butch Cassidy in a scene from the 1969 film *Butch Cassidy and the Sundance Kid*. *John Springer Collection/Corbis*

## PLAYING GANGS FOR LAUGHS

Hollywood has a long tradition of laughing at difficult problems, and gangs are no exception. A prime example is the "Bowery Boys" series, presenting a group of tough (but ultimately harmless) young hoodlums who wisecracked their way through 51 comic adventures spanning 20 years.

Titles in the comic series include *Angels with Dirty Faces* (1938), *Bowery Boy* (1940), *Bowery Bombshell* (1946), *Hard Boiled Mahoney* (1947), *Trouble Makers* (1948), *Bowery Battalion* (1951), and *Fighting Trouble* (1956).

## ⚲ SHAKESPEARE IN GANGLAND

Modern students sometimes complain that they "don't understand" the classic works of William Shakespeare (1564–1616) taught in high school English classes, but his plays contain themes that are common to life throughout human history. A case in point is *Romeo and Juliet*, the story of two teenagers from feuding families who fall in love against their parents' wishes and come to a tragic end, thus teaching their elders the folly of hatred.

In fact, *Romeo and Juliet* is so timeless that it has been adapted three times for modern stage and screen, presenting its characters (sometimes with different names) as members and victims of modern street-gang culture.

The first modern retelling of Shakespeare's classic, *West Side Story* (1961), transports the tale to New York City, where two rival gangs—the Jets and Sharks—battle for turf and respect. Racism further tints the story, since the Sharks are Puerto Rican and the Jets are "native" whites. Tony is a former leader of the Jets who falls in love with Maria, sister of boss-Shark Bernardo. Their fate is preordained in this classic Hollywood musical that won eight Academy Awards (including Best Picture of the Year) in 1962.

The theme of racial conflict is repeated in *China Girl* (1987), as another Tony with gang connections finds himself smitten with Tye, the sister of a Chinese gangster in New York City. Once again, the forbidden romance strains friendships and family ties, drawing the characters relentlessly toward violent confrontation and death.

Shakespeare's original title and poetic dialogue remain in Hollywood's 1996 version, *Romeo + Juliet*, but the star-crossed lovers are transplanted from sixteenth-century Verona, Italy, to fictional "Verona Beach," where gangs armed with modern weapons cruise the streets in flashy, souped-up cars. The end result remains an epic tragedy, with gunfire in place of swordplay.

Meanwhile, comic actor Jerry Lewis dropped into gangland for *The Delicate Delinquent* (1957). Bumbling outlaw bikers pursued Clint Eastwood in *Every Which Way But Loose* (1978) and *Any Which Way You Can* (1980). After a successful Broadway run, high school hoodlums turned musical in *Grease* (1978) and *Grease 2* (1982). All were successful at the box office, but individuals involved with real-life gangs occasionally missed the joke.

## REBELS WITHOUT A CAUSE

In the 1950s J. Edgar Hoover warned America of danger from a growing "army" of juvenile gangsters. That fear was aggravated by films including James Dean's classic *Rebel Without a Cause* (1955), *Cry Tough* (1959), and *The Choppers* (1961)—advertised with posters screaming: "Young Lives Wasted!" Each portrayed a teenage generation lost to mindless thrills and violence, chasing "kicks" on a dead-end road.

Outlaw bikers made their screen debut in *The Wild One* (1953), but another decade passed before Hells Angels and their rivals took Hollywood by storm. Movies attempting to portray the 1-percenter lifestyle include *The Wild Angels* (1966), *Hells Angels on Wheels* (1967), *The Cycle Savages* (1969), *Hells Angels '69* (1969), *Angels Die Hard* (1970), and *Hells Angels Forever* (1983).

## LIFE MIRRORS ART

In 1977 *Time* magazine ran a cover story on "The Godfather Syndrome," reporting that a series of Hollywood films based on Mario Puzo's Mafia novel *The Godfather* had changed the way real-life Italian gangsters behaved in their daily lives. Some members of the Mafia (or *Cosa Nostra*, meaning "Our Thing" in Italian) began to dress and talk in imitation of *Godfather* stars Marlon Brando, Al Pacino, and Robert DeNiro. Police sources even reported that one of New York City's most prominent mobsters, Carlo Gambino, ordered a band to play theme music from *The Godfather* when he entered a banquet room.

While that behavior may seem comic, the *Godfather* novel and films also seemingly encouraged some Italian mobsters to believe that they controlled all organized crime in the United States—a

Al Pacino as Michael Corleone and Marlon Brando as Vito Corleone in Francis Ford Coppola's *The Godfather*. *Sunset Boulevard/Corbis*

fact disputed both by law enforcement leaders and by rival, non-Italian gangs who took violent issue with increased bullying from conceited neighborhood "bosses."

In *Paddy Whacked*, a 2005 history of Irish gangsters in America, author T. J. English recounts some of the conflicts that erupted between Irish and Italian gangs when Mafia members obsessed with "The Godfather Syndrome" invaded neighborhoods where non-Italian gangsters held control. Resulting battles in Boston, Cleveland, and elsewhere claimed dozens of lives.

## THAT WAS THEN...

Since the early 1980s, Hollywood has approached the subject of gangs more seriously. S. E. Hinton's classic novels hit the big screen during 1983–85: *Tex, The Outsiders, Rumble Fish,* and *That Was Then, This Is Now.* Other screenwriters focused on gang history and the rise of specific gangs. *Gangs of New York* (2002) revisited the late nineteenth century, while *American Me* (1992), written by Floyd Mutrux, charted the rise of the Mexican Mafia. *American History X* (1998) examined neo-Nazi skinheads. *Scarface* (1983) traced the growth of Cuban and Colombian drug syndicates in America. *Bad Boys* (1983) took viewers inside an urban reform school, while *Switchblade Sisters* (1975) portrayed a female gang. Ghetto sets spawned films including *Colors* (1988), *Boyz n the Hood* (1991), *Menace II Society* (1993), and *Strapped* (1993).

At the other end of the spectrum, Walter Hill's surrealistic film *The Warriors* (1979), based on Sol Yurick's novel, prompted real-life gangsters to brawl in theaters from New York to Los Angeles. Futuristic gangs with science-fiction overtones appeared in *A Clockwork Orange* (1971), *Streets of Fire* (1984), and *Class of 1999* (1990). The bottom line for Hollywood was still the bottom line: profits, with just a hint of social education in the mix.

Today, *Scarface* (1980), directed by Brian DePalma and starring Al Pacino, enjoys a resurgence in popularity. The film's depiction of Tony Montana, a Cuban immigrant who rises to wealth and power as the violent leader of a drug gang, apparently resonates with audiences who favor gangsta rap and depictions of gangsta culture.

# Coping with Gangs

Murder. Rape. Assault. Armed robbery. Carjacking. Burglary. Drug dealing. Prostitution. Human trafficking. Arson and bombing. Kidnapping. Torture. Bribery. Extortion. Fraud. Witness intimidation. Jury tampering.

The list of crimes committed every day by gangs in the United States seems endless. Parents and police, teachers and lawmakers, officials from the White House down to small-town City Halls, all seek solutions for the problem that has turned into a plague. Unfortunately, while most people have opinions on the best way to get rid of violent gangs, agreement on one method—and its funding—is elusive.

There are two broad schools of thought on how to deal with gangs. One method, intervention, seeks to educate gang members or potential recruits and distract them from crime with other activities. The alternative, suppression, stresses hard-line punishment of gang-related crimes. Most cities in America today combine the two approaches without great success.

## GANG INTERVENTION

Organized efforts to divert young gangsters from antisocial behavior began in the nineteenth century, with ministers attempting to convert and "save" urban delinquents. Soon, Police Athletic Leagues were formed to "build character" through sports and improve police–community relations. While both programs had some success, gangs continued to grow and become more violent.

Los Angeles, with its high rate of gang-related murders since the 1970s, pioneered modern gang prevention efforts with its L.A.

Participants in the Police Athletic League's summer day camp play in an open fire hydrant. The league was formed to keep kids away from gangs and improve community–police relations. *AP Photo/ Mary Altaffer*

Bridges Program. As described on its Web site (http://www.lacity. org/cdd/lab_prev.html), L.A. Bridges includes both prevention and intervention techniques. Prevention efforts for children displaying high-risk characteristics of future gang involvement include

- individual and family counseling
- anger management and conflict resolution classes
- tutoring and help with homework
- parenting activities and family outings

- job training and placement
- neighborhood clean-up campaigns
- organized sports and other recreational activities

L.A. Bridges intervention teams work with gang members to reduce ongoing violence in various ways. Aside from the same education, job training, and anger-management courses offered to gang prospects, the teams try to

- create and maintain truces between rival gangs
- mediate in crisis situations
- assist with tattoo removal
- schedule "scared straight" visits to prisons
- conduct graffiti-removal campaigns
- organize peace marches and rallies
- negotiate restitution to gang victims

While most gang-prevention programs celebrate their own success, many critics still have doubts. They note that truces in Los Angeles and other cities have not lasted long, and even when in place, they simply freed gangsters participating in the truce to sell more drugs or prey on other local gangs.

The answer, say those critics, is to lock all gangsters up and throw away the key.

## RICO

In 1970, Congress passed a law designed to do exactly that. The Racketeer Influenced and Corrupt Organizations Act (shortened to *RICO*) increases penalties for various crimes, such as murder, arson, robbery, or extortion, when the offender belongs to an organized criminal group. Some reporters claim the RICO Act was named for Rico, the main gangster in the film *Little Caesar* (1931), but authors of the law refuse to confirm or deny it.

RICO lists 35 specific crimes, stating that any group or person who commits two or more within a 10-year period may be charged with racketeering. If convicted, a defendant may serve 20 years in prison (with a $25,000 fine) on each charge, *and* must forfeit all money or property gained through criminal activity. Private victims of racketeering may also sue the offenders for triple damages.

RICO offenses include arson, bribery, counterfeiting, dealing in controlled substances or obscene matter, embezzlement, extortion, fraud, gambling, illegal transactions with labor unions, immigration violations, kidnapping, loan-sharking, money laundering, murder, obstruction of justice, robbery, securities fraud, theft, and witness intimidation.

While RICO has sent many gangsters, drug dealers, and leaders of organized crime off to prison, prosecution is not limited to

## GANGS VS. SYNDICATES

When is a gang not a gang? Definitions of the term, like most language used in law enforcement, have changed over time. Before the 1930s, most criminal organizations were called "gangs," regardless of their size or the age of their members. Examples include the "Capone Gang" in Chicago and Detroit's bootlegging "Purple Gang." Today, however, organized crime groups are commonly described as "syndicates," "mobs," or "cartels," while the gang label is reserved for groups of younger offenders engaged in "disorganized" crime.

Problems arise when street or motorcycle gangs grow large, wealthy, and powerful through drug dealing and other criminal pursuits. Most law enforcement agencies today recognize the old 1960s motorcycle gangs as part of organized crime, with operations spanning the United States and other nations. Some official spokesmen distinguish newer syndicates by labeling older gangs (such as the Sicilian Mafia) as "traditional organized crime" groups.

Two prime examples of graduation from mere "gang" status to syndicate levels are the Hells Angels and the Crips. Both began, in their own ways, as local gangs devoted to hard partying and "rumbling" with rival cliques for territory or respect. Today, both are recognized as multimillion-dollar operations, involved in organized criminal activity including drug trafficking, prostitution, sale of illegal weapons, and contract murders. In some parts of the United States, motorcycle gangs or inner-city street gangs have replaced "traditional" gangs as the dominant forces in organized crime.

obvious criminal groups like the Crips or the Mafia. In SLAPP cases (strategic *l*awsuit *a*gainst *p*ublic *p*articipation), charges may be filed against persons who sue crime victims or corporate whistleblowers to keep them quiet or punish them for revealing criminal activity.

In 1986, the National Organization for Women filed a RICO lawsuit against two "pro life" groups that blockaded American abortion clinics and threatened violence against staff members. Seventeen years later, federal courts declared that RICO offenses must involve some financial motive. Religious or political conspiracies are not covered, unless they somehow involve money.

In 2003, minority owners of the Montréal Expos baseball team filed RICO complaints against Major League Baseball, claiming a conspiracy to devalue the team before a move. In 2005, after extensive arbitration, the case was settled for an undisclosed sum and the Expos moved to Washington.

## EARS AND EYES INSIDE

Before prosecutors can file any charges, they need evidence. Of course, gangs often operate in secret or use stolen, disposable weapons for public shootings. Witnesses to crimes are bribed, threatened, or killed. Confessions will convict gang members, but obtaining them is often difficult.

With special search warrants, police may *tap* telephone lines, plant hidden listening devices, or read private letters and e-mail to find evidence of a crime. Dramatic recordings of conversations including murder plots and other crimes have convicted many gang leaders, including New York Mafia boss John Gotti. However, as high-tech listening devices become more sophisticated, so gangsters become more cautious.

Eyewitness testimony is more dramatic than audiotapes—and more dangerous. Some law enforcement agencies train officers to infiltrate criminal groups, posing as loyal members while they collect evidence to destroy the gang and imprison its members. Famous undercover agents include

- James McParland, an Irishman who came to America at age 24 (in 1867) and joined the Pinkerton Detective Agency four years later. In 1873, he infiltrated the Molly Maguires, a terrorist

Surveillance equipment used by law enforcement officials to investigate gangs. *Adrianna Williams/zefa/Corbis*

group that waged guerrilla war against Pennsylvania's top coal-mining companies. By 1876, McParland compiled evidence in 50 murders and many other cases, sending 20 defendants to the gallows.

- Joseph Pistone, an FBI agent who infiltrated one of New York City's five Mafia families in the 1970s, working closely with various mobsters for six years. While never actually inducted as a *made* (oath-bound) Mafia member, Pistone still gathered evidence resulting in 100 felony convictions. Mobsters put a $50,000 murder contract on Pistone, but later canceled it under threats from the FBI. Actor Johnny Depp portrayed Pistone in the film *Donnie Brasco* (1997).

■ William Queen, an agent for the Bureau of Alcohol, Tobacco, Firearms and Explosives, infiltrated the violent Mongol Nation motorcycle gang in 1998, as biker "Billy St. John." Over the next 28 months, Queen gathered evidence of murder, weapons, and drug violations, sending various gang members to prison. In 2005, Queen published the memoir *Under and Alone*.

Where a gang's "blood in, blood out" philosophy prevents police officers from joining the group, civilian informants often prove useful. Two types of criminal informants are (a) those that confess after being arrested, in hopes of lenient treatment; and (b) those still active in the gang, cooperating in return for money or favors. Famous examples of the first type include

■ Abraham "Kid Twist" Reles (1906–41), a mob hitman who exposed the workings of "Murder, Incorporated" after his arrest for homicide in 1939. His testimony sent several other contract killers to death row. On November 12, 1941, Reles fell from a hotel window while guarded by six detectives. Police called his death an accident, but mob boss Lucky Luciano later claimed officers were paid $50,000 to kill Reles.

■ Joseph Valachi (1903–71), another New York gangster, imprisoned on drug charges, who broke the Sicilian code of silence, or *omertá*, after Mafia boss Vito Genovese tried to kill him in 1963. Valachi's testimony confirmed testimony from Reles and sparked public fascination with the Mafia, inspiring the *Godfather* novel and films.

■ Henry Hill (1943–   ), a gangster linked to the Mafia who turned informer after his arrest on drug charges. His testimony sent various high-level mobsters to prison. Actor Ray Liotta played Hill in the movie *Goodfellas* (1990).

In the 1960s and 1970s FBI agents maintained a large network of active informants in various political groups suspected of criminal activity. Some, like Alabama Ku Klux Klan member Gary Rowe, provided testimony that sent terrorists to prison. Others, like some assigned to the Black Panther Party, arranged events where subjects died under suspicious circumstances. In most such cases, defense attorneys charge that informants have lied or fabricated false evidence to earn their paychecks or to escape prosecution for crimes of their own.

## WITNESS SECURITY

In 1970 the federal government created a Witness Security Program (WITSEC) to shelter witnesses threatened by retaliation from

Joseph Valachi, convicted murderer and *Cosa Nostra* mobster, testifies before the Senate Permanent Investigation Committee in Washington, D.C., on his involvement in the Mafia. *AP Photo*

dangerous criminals or gangs. Over the past four decades, agents of the U.S. Marshals Service have concealed and guarded more than 7,500 witnesses and nearly 10,000 family members.

## ⚲ BREAKING UNIT 88

The Arizona skinhead gang called Unit 88 took its name from the eighth letter of the alphabet—*H*—doubled to stand for *Heil Hitler*. Its 37 hard-drinking members collected weapons, robbed homes, and sold drugs to support themselves. They also killed at least two victims before detective Matt Browning broke up the gang.

Starting in 1996, Browning infiltrated various hate groups including the Aryan Nations, Ku Klux Klan, National Alliance, and Unit 88. In October 2002, after three gang members killed an African-American man outside a Phoenix pool hall, Browning identified the slayers by their tattoos and tracked them to the rural hideout where they were captured. Trial on capital charges was pending in that case when this book went to press.

In another case, Unit 88 members murdered freshcut (rookie) member Jeremy Johnson for stealing money from a female member's purse. Police found Johnson's bones in the desert, and Browning identified the killers, who later bragged about their crime, leading to their arrests in September 2003.

Josh Fielder, leader of Unit 88, received a 10-year sentence for robbery in 2004, again thanks to Browning. Fielder wore a ski mask during the invasion of a Phoenix home where money, drugs, and guns were stolen, but he failed to cover tattoos on his neck. He was shocked when Browning arrested him.

Browning and the FBI were building a RICO case against the neo-Nazi National Alliance, which used Unit 88 as its "enforcement arm" in Arizona, when leaders quarreled and the group splintered. In 1978 National Alliance founder William Luther Pierce (1933–2002) published *The Turner Diaries*, a racist novel that inspired terrorist Timothy McVeigh (1968–2001) to bomb Oklahoma City's Alfred P. Murrah Federal Building in April 1995, killing 168 persons. The same book also inspired members of The Order, another white supremacist group, to commit various robberies and murders during 1983–84.

The process involves creation of new identities and relocation to areas where the witnesses are unknown. Most of those hidden by WITSEC have testified against members of organized crime, gangs such as the Crips or Hells Angels, or terrorist groups like the Ku Klux Klan. Protected witnesses must cut all ties with their former lives, but the strain proves too much for some, and a few who returned to their hometowns have been murdered in retaliation for their testimony.

Various states, starting with California and New York, have created their own WITSEC programs on the federal model, but they have smaller budgets and limited jurisdiction, generally providing security only within their own borders.

## PROBLEMS WITH INFORMANTS

Throughout history, criminal informants have caused trouble for law enforcement agencies worldwide. The obvious problem in dealing with felons is trying to keep them honest. Investigators must always ask themselves if informants are lying or faking evidence to increase their payoffs, to please their police handlers and gain favors, to protect themselves from prosecution, or to settle some personal grudge.

One ever-present danger with informants is the risk of entrapment, defined as a situation where police or their agents persuade otherwise innocent persons to commit a crime. American courts reject the entrapment defense if those on trial were ready and willing to participate in crime (like known drug dealers or thieves), but jurors may feel otherwise in some cases. Federal prosecutors lost several big cases in the 1960s and 1970s because FBI informants had supplied illegal weapons or bombs to various "radical" groups and suggested acts of terrorism.

Simple greed is another problem with informants, who normally receive more money when their testimony produces arrests and convictions. In some RICO cases, prosecution witnesses also share in cash or other valuables seized from convicted defendants. In 1991–92 alone, the Justice Department's Assets Forfeiture Fund paid $46 million to criminal informants nationwide.

Informants often escape prosecution for various crimes by turning against their gangster friends. In 1965, Massachusetts hitman

Joseph "The Animal" Barboza falsely accused four innocent defendants of a murder he committed. The four received life sentences and two died in prison. The other two served 25 years before they were freed. By that time, Barboza was dead, killed by an assassin, despite his placement in the WITSEC program.

Another Mafia killer, Salvatore "Sammy the Bull" Gravano, confessed to 19 murders but avoided prosecution by turning infor-

## ♀ "STOP SNITCHIN'"

In late 2004, Baltimore record producer Rodney Thomas (presently serving 15 years for first-degree assault) produced a DVD titled "Stop Snitchin'" that included threats from alleged drug dealers against persons who testify in criminal cases. Carmelo Anthony, a Baltimore native and professional basketball player for the Denver Nuggets, also appeared on the video, but later claimed that his participation was "a joke." Primary targets of the "Stop Snitchin'" DVD were drug offenders who testify against accomplices in order to reduce their own jail sentences.

Baltimore police responded to the video with their own "Keep Talkin'" campaign, but the "Stop Snitchin'" effort soon spread nationwide. T-shirts sold in various cities across the United States display stop signs with the "Stop Snitchin'" logo, some of the signs including bullet holes implying that informants will be killed.

In Boston, where the T-shirts first appeared in 1999, Mayor Thomas Menino ordered police to confiscate the garments, and officers pressured stores to stop selling them. Five years later, after a Boston gang member's mother wore a "Stop Snitchin'" shirt to her son's murder trial, various cities banned display of the shirts in courtrooms.

Public reaction to the "Stop Snitchin'" campaign has been mixed. While rival "Start Snitchin'" and "STOP Stop Snitchin'" T-shirts are also available, rap star Immortal Technique insists that black and Hispanic Americans should not "snitch" on ghetto criminals until police officers begin informing on each other for bribery, brutality, and other illegal actions.

mant against boss John Gotti and others. Gravano left WITSEC in 1995 and settled in Arizona, where police charged him with drug trafficking in February 2000. Jurors convicted Gravano in October 2002, and he received a 19-year sentence.

# Chronology

**1790s**    *New York City:* Early street gangs organized.

**1825**    *New York City:* The 40 Thieves operate from New York's first speakeasy, in the Five Points district.

**1830**    *New York City:* The Dead Rabbits organize after a rift in the Roach Guards.

**1834**    *New York City:* An anti-Catholic gang calling itself The Native Americans joins in a three-day riot protesting extension of suffrage to Irishmen.

**1849**    *May*   *New York City:* Five Points gangsters riot to protest an English actor's performance, leaving 31 dead and 140 injured.

**1863**    *July*   *New York City:* Gang members kill hundreds of blacks during racist draft riots.

**1866**    *February*   *Liberty, Mo.:* The James-Younger gang stages America's first daylight bank robbery.

**1868**    *December*   *New Albany, Ind.:* Vigilantes lynch four leaders of the Reno gang.

**1892**    *October 5*   *Coffeyville, Kan.:* Townspeople wipe out the Dalton gang.

**1900**    *New York City:* Police investigate the first of several "tong" wars between rival Chinese gangs.

**1903**    *August*   *New York City:* Five-Pointers battle Eastmans in the city's largest-ever gun battle, while Gophers join in and shoot at both sides.

**1919**    *July*   *Chicago:* White street gangs join in a race riot, leaving 38 dead and 537 injured.

**1929**    *February*   *Chicago:* Seven North Side gang members die in the St. Valentine's Day massacre.

**1934**    *April*   *Rhinelander, Wisc.:* Two persons die in an FBI shootout with the Dillinger gang.

**1942**    *Chicago:* Almighty Latin King Nation organized.

**1943** *June   Los Angeles:* U.S. servicemen attack supposed Latino gang members in a series of "zoot suit riots."

**1948** *March   San Bernardino, Calif.:* Hells Angels motorcycle gang organized.

**1956** *California:* Hispanic prison inmates form the Mexican Mafia.

**1959** *Chicago:* Outlaws motorcycle gang and Blackstone Rangers street gang organized.

*August   New York City:* Members of three Puerto Rican gangs kill two white youths at a Hell's Kitchen playground.

**1966** *San Quentin, Calif.:* Black Guerrilla Family founded.

*March   Houston, Tex.:* Bandidos motorcycle gang created.

**1967** *San Quentin, Calif.:* Aryan Brotherhood organized.

*Chicago:* The Blackstone Rangers become the first street gang to expand beyond their founding "turf" to other cities.

**1968** *New York City:* Irish hoodlums organize the Westies in Hell's Kitchen.

**1969** *December   Los Angeles:* Crips street gang founded at Fremont High School.

**1972** *Los Angeles:* Bloods street gang organized in opposition to Crips.

*New York City:* Members of the Savage Skulls and the Savage Nomads kill two addicts while "protecting" their South Bronx turf.

**1974** *United States:* Hells Angels and Outlaws begin a nationwide gang war that continues today.

*Los Angeles:* 74 gang-related murders investigated.

*May   Los Angeles:* Five members of the Symbionese Liberation Army die in a shootout with police.

**1974–75** *Pennsylvania:* A gang war between the Pagans and Warlocks claims 15 lives.

**1978** *United States:* Bandidos and Outlaws form an alliance for drug distribution.

**1980** *Los Angeles:* 355 gang-related murders reported.

**1984**   *November*   *Idaho:* Members of The Order declare war on the U.S. government.

**1985**   *June*   *Quebec:* Hells Angels kill five of their own gang members in a dispute over drugs.

**1986**   *August*   *Chicago:* FBI agents charge El Rukns gang members with participation in a Libyan terrorist plot.

**1989**   *New York City:* The Chinese Flying Dragons gang battles for turf against the Vietnamese BTK (Born to Kill).

**1992**   *April*   *Los Angeles:* Crips and Bloods declare a national truce.

**1996**   *New York City:* Black inmates at Rikers Island form the United Blood Nation to oppose the Latin Kings.

**2001**   *March*   *Canada:* Police jail 120 outlaw bikers in "Operation Springtime."

**2002**   *May*   *Montreal:* Hells Angels leader Maurice Boucher receives a life sentence for ordering murders of two prison guards in 1997.

**2005**   *December*   *San Quentin, Calif.:* Crips leader "Tookie" Williams dies by lethal injection for murders committed in 1979.

**2006**   *April*   *Shedden, Ontario:* "Internal cleansing" claims the lives of five Bandidos gang members.

# Endnotes

**Chapter 1**

1. Paul Lunde, *Organized Crime* (London: DK, 2004), 121.

**Chapter 4**

1. Yves Lavigne, *Hell's Angels* (New York: Lyle Stuart, 1996), 79–80.

**Chapter 7**

1. Morris Dees, *Hate on Trial* (New York: Villard Books, 1993), 269–73.

# Bibliography

Anbinder, Tyler. *Five Points*. New York: Plume, 2002.

Asbury, Herbert. *The Gangs of Chicago: An Informal History of the Chicago Underworld*. New York: Thunder's Mouth Press, 2002.

_____. *The Gangs of New York: An Informal History of the Underworld*. New York: Thunder's Mouth Press, 2001.

Bing, Leon. *Do or Die*. New York: Harper Perennial, 1992.

Buchanan, Susy. "Breaking the Skins." *Intelligence Report* 121 (Spring 2006): 23–29.

Christensen, Loren. *Gangbangers: Understanding The Deadly Minds of America's Street Gangs*. Boulder, Colo.: Paladin Press, 1999.

Gale, William. *The Compound*. New York: Rawson Associates, 1977.

Lavigne, Yves. *Hells Angels: Into the Abyss*. Secaucus, N.J.: Lyle Stuart, 1996.

Morton, James. *Gangland Today*. London: Time Warner, 2005.

Sanchez, Reymundo. *My Bloody Life: The Making of a Latin King*. Chicago: Chicago Review Press, 2001.

Shakur, Sanyika. *Monster: The Autobiography of an L.A. Gang Member*. New York: Grove Press, 2004.

Sher, Julian, and William Marsden. *Angels of Death: Inside the Biker Gangs' Crime Empire*. New York: Carroll & Graff, 2006.

Sikes, Gini. *8 Ball Chicks*. New York: Anchor, 1998.

Simpson, Colton, and Ann Pearlman. *Inside the Crips: Life Inside L.A.'s Most Notorious Gang*. New York: St. Martin's Press, 2005.

Valentine, Bill. *Gangs and Their Tattoos: Identifying Gangbangers on the Street and in Prison*. Boulder, Colo.: Paladin Press, 2000.

Veno, Arthur. *The Brotherhoods: Inside the Outlaw Motorcycle Clubs*. Sydney, Australia: Allen & Unwin, 2004.

Vigil, Diego. *A Rainbow of Gangs: Street Cultures in the Mega-City*. Austin: University of Texas Press, 2002.

# Further Resources

## Books

Jackson, Robert, and Wesley McBride. *Understanding Street Gangs.* Belmont, Calif.: Wadsworth Publishing, 2000.

Morton, James. *Gangland International: The Mafia and Other Mobs.* London: Warner Books, 1998.

Valentine, Bill. *Gang Intelligence Manual.* Boulder, Colo.: Paladin Press, 1985.

## Web Sites

Gang and Security Threat Group Awareness
http://www.dc.state.fl.us/pub/gangs/index.html

Gangs or Us
http://www.gangsorus.com/index.html

Into the Abyss
http://www.faculty.missouristate.edu/M/MichaelCarlie/default.htm

Know Gangs
http://www.knowgangs.com/

National Youth Gang Center
http://www.iir.com/nygc

Prison Gangs
http://www.tgia.net/Links/Information_Sites/Prison_Gangs/prison_gangs.html

Street Gangs Resource Center
http://www.streetgangs.com

# Index

Page numbers in *italics* indicate images.

**A**

"ABC." *See* American-born Chinese

Abel 8

Administrative Maximum (ADX) prison 63, *63*, 64

ADX prison. *See* Administrative Maximum prison

African ethnic gangs 78–80

Albanian Boys Incorporated 78

alcohol, ban on. *See* Prohibition era

American-born Chinese (ABC) 74

*American History X* 89

*American Me* (Mutrux) 89

American Motorcycle Association 49

*America's Most Wanted* 75

amphetamines 30

Anderson, William 53

*Angels Die Hard* 87

*Angels with Dirty Faces* 86

Annihilators 47

Anslinger, Harry 28

Anthony, Carmelo 101

*Any Which Way You Can* 87

arson 13

Aryan Brotherhood 56, 58, 59, 61, 62

Aryan Nations 58, 81, 99

Asian Boyz 75, 77

Asian ethnic gangs 30, 73–75

ATF. *See* Bureau of Alcohol, Tobacco, Firearms and Explosives

Avenue Cribs. *See* Baby Avenues

**B**

Baby Avenues 65

*Bad Boys* 89

ballistics markings 26–27

Bandido Nation. *See* Bandidos Motorcycle Club

Bandidos Motorcycle Club 47, 48, 51, 52, 53

bank robberies 37–38

Barboza, Joseph "The Animal" 101

Barker, "Ma" 84

Barrow, Clyde 37

Bates, Albert 42–43

*Before Night Falls* 75

BGF. *See* Black Guerrilla Family

Big Four motorcycle gangs 49–52, 53

"Big Seven" 28

Bingham, Stephen 57

Black Guerrilla Family (BGF) 56–58, 59

Black Hand 19–20

black liberation 57

Black Liberation Army 58

Black Muslims 65

Black Panther Party 57, 65, 98

Black Vanguard. *See* Black Guerrilla Family

"Bleeding Kansas" 18

"blood in, blood out" 56, 62, 97

Blood Kills 66

*Blood in My Eye* (Jackson) 57

Bloods 14, 61, 65–72

*Blue Rage, Black Redemption* (Williams) 67

boat people and ethnic gangs 75–76, *76*

Bonham, Frank 84

Bonney, William "Billy the Kid" 84

*Bonnie and Clyde* 37
books, gangs and gang crime portrayed in 83–84, 87, 89. *See also specific books*
bootleggers 12, 13, 23–33, 84, 94
boot parties. *See* group stompings
Boozefighter Motorcycle Club 48, 49
"bopping" 12
Born to Kill (BTK) 74
Boston, MA 11, 28, 89, 101
*Bowery Battalion* 86
*Bowery Bombshell* 86
*Bowery Boy* 86
"Bowery Boys" series 85–86
Bowman, Harry 49–50
*Boyz n the Hood* 89
Brando, Marlon 48, 87, 88, *88*
Brasscatcher (cartridge case identification program) 27
Brighton Beach (New York) 78
British Knight athletic shoes 66
Bronx (New York City, NY) 78
Brotherhood of the Chosen 81
Brown, Foxy 71
Browning, Matt 99
BTK. *See* Born to Kill
"Bugs." *See* Moran, George "Bugs"
Bulletproof (bullet identification program) 27
Bureau of Alcohol, Tobacco, Firearms and Explosives (ATF) 26, 54, 97
Burke, Fred "Killer" 26
Bush, George H. W. 31–32
Bush, George W. 67
*Butch Cassidy and the Sundance Kid* 40, 84, 85, *85*
Byrd, James, Jr. 58

**C**
Cain 8
Camorra 19
Capone, Al ("Scarface") 12, 26, 35, 36, *36*
Capone, Ralph 35

Capone Gang 94
Capone-N-Noreaga 71
"Captain Lightfoot" 12
"Captain Thunderbolt" 12
cartels 94
Carver, Bill 39, *39*
Cassidy, Butch. *See* Parker, Robert LeRoy
Castro, Fidel 75
Chambers, Donald Eugene 52
Chicago, IL
  "Black Hand" practice 19
  Crime Commission 35–37
  growth of gangs and gang crime in 18
  motorcycle gangs 49
  Prohibition era in 25, 26–27, 94
Chichesters 17
*China Girl* 86
*The Choppers* 87
Christian Identity 81
*Chung Ching Yee* 73
*Class of 1999* 89
Cleveland, OH 89
*A Clockwork Orange* 89
cocaine 29–30, 68
code of silence 97
Colombian gangs 29, 89
*Colors* 89
colors, gang 50–51, 56, 59
Colosimo, "Big Jim" 27
Connecticut White Wolves 81
Consolidated Crip Organization 61, 66
"Contra" guerrillas 32
Cook, Fred 13
Coppola, Francis Ford 88
*Cosa Nostra. See* Mafia
crack 68–69
crank. *See* crystal methamphetamine
crime. *See also* gangs and gang crime
  effect on everyone 7
  statistics on 7
  types of gang — 12–13

Crips  14, 61, 65–72, 75, 77, 94, 95, 100
"Cripwalk"  69, 72
crossburning  79
crystal methamphetamine  52
*Cry Tough*  87
Cuban gangs  75, 89
Cummings, Homer  35
Curry, Kid  39, *39*
"C-walk." *See* "Cripwalk"
*The Cycle Savages*  87

**D**

Dalton brothers  18–19, 37, 84
Damu Ridaz  72
Daniel (prophet)  8
Dasilva, Jesse  72
Davis, Angela  57
Daz Dillinger  69
DEA. *See* Drug Enforcement Agency
Dead Rabbits  16, 17
Dean, James  87
Death Row Records  71, 72
*The Delicate Delinquent*  87
"Demon Run"  23
DeNiro, Robert  87
Denver Nuggets  101
DePalma, Brian  89
Depp, Johnny  97
Detroit, MI  25, 94
Dillinger, John  35–36, 39, 43–44, *44*, 84
*Dillinger: Dead or Alive?* (Nash)  44
Dirty White Boys  61
Disney studios, Walt  52
DJ Quick  72
Dobkins, Louis  52
Dobyns, Jay  54
*Donnie Brasco*  97
Draper, Sharon  84
drive-by shootings  66, 70
"Drop It Like It's Hot"  72
"Drug Czar"  29
drug dealers  13

Drug Enforcement Agency (DEA)  29, 31, 54
DRUGFIRE  26–27
drug wars  28–30
*Durango Street* (Bonham)  84

**E**

Eastern European ethnic gangs  78
Eastman, Monk  12
Eastmans  17
East Side White Pride  79
Eastwood, Clint  87
Eazy-E  69
18th Amendment  25
elections, rigging  17–18
Ellison, Harlan  84
El Rukns  13
England, Dominique  55
English, T. J.  89
entertainment, gangs and gang crime as  12
entrapment  100
ethnic gangs
  African  78–80
  Asian  73–75
  boat people  75–76, *76*
  Filipino  77–78
  Jamaican posses  76–77
  Russian/Eastern European  78
  skinhead groups  81
*Every Which Way But Loose*  87
extortion  19
eyewitness testimony  95

**F**

family, gang as substitute  11–12
FBI. *See* Federal Bureau of Investigation
FBN. *See* Federal Bureau of Narcotics
Federal Bureau of Investigation (FBI)
  ballistics network  26–27
  drug seizure reports  29
  most wanted list  50

organized-crime investigations
    31
policing of motorcycle gangs
    54
public enemies list  35
Federal Bureau of Narcotics (FBN)
    28
Federal-Wide Drug Seizure System
    29
Fielder, Josh  99
*Fighting Trouble*  86
Filipino ethnic gangs  77–78
Filipino Mafia. *See* Vargas Family
films, gangs and gang crime por-
    trayed in  84–89. *See also spe-
    cific films*
"Five Points" district (New York
    City, NY)  16–17, *17*
Five Points Gang  16–17
Floyd, Charles "Pretty Boy"  41, *41*,
    42, 84
"FOB." *See* fresh off the boat
Folsom Prison (California)  60
forensic evidence  27
Forkner, "Wino Willie"  48
Fort Sumter (Charleston, SC)  18
Fox, Brian  40
Foxx, Jamie  67
fresh off the boat (FOB)  74
Fresno, CA  75
Fritos corn chips  52
Fula, Yafeu  71
"full-patch" outlaw biker members
    50

**G**
Gambino, Carlo  87
gambling, illegal  13
gangs and gang crime
    books, — portrayed in  83–84,
        87, 89. *See also specific
        books*
    bootleg operations  23–33
    bylaws of  12
    defined  94
    as entertainment  12
    ethnic —  73–81

films, — portrayed in  84–89.
    *See also specific films*
ghetto gangs  65–72
growth of  15–21
history of  11
initiation rituals  12
law enforcement efforts to sup-
    press  91–102
leaders, role of  12
motorcycle gangs  47–54
newspapers, — portrayed in
    12
prison gangs  55–64, *60*
psychological description of
    11–12
public enemies and holdup
    gangs  35–45, 84
as substitute families  11–12
types of —  12–13
vs. syndicates  94
*Gangs of New York*  16, 89
gangsta rap  69–72, 89
gangster weapons  45
Genovese, Vito  97
ghetto gangs  65–72, 89
Ghost Shadows  74
G-men (government men)  42
*The Godfather* (book; Puzo)  87,
    97
*The Godfather* (film)  87–89, *88*,
    97
"The Godfather Syndrome"  87, 89
Gonzo journalism  49
*Goodfellas*  97
Gotti, John  95, 102
government men. *See* G-men
Gravano, Salvatore "Sammy the
    Bull"  101–102
*Grease*  87
*Grease 2*  87
group stompings  81

**H**
Haiti  75–76
*Hard Boiled Mahoney*  86
Harding, Warren  25
Harrelson, Charles  52

Harrelson, Woody  52
hate crime  55, 65, 79
Hearst, Patty  58
Hegel, Georg  30
Hells Angels  47, 49, 50–53, 54, 87,
    94, 100
*Hell's Angels* (book; Thompson)  49
*Hells Angels* (movie)  50
*Hells Angels Forever*  87
*Hells Angels on Wheels*  87
*Hells Angels 69*  87
Hennessy, David  20
heroin  29–30
"highwaymen"  11, 12
Highway 61 gang  53
Hill, Henry  97
Hill, Walter  89
Hinton, S. E.  83–84, 89
Hitler, Adolf  58
Hmong  75
holdup gangs  35–45
Hole-in-the-Wall (Wyoming hide-
    out)  39, 84
Hot 97 studios  71
Hoover, J. Edgar  28, 35, 38, 42, 87
human trafficking  13

**I**

IBIS. *See* Integrated Ballistics Iden-
    tification System
ice. *See* crystal methamphetamine
Ice-T  72
immigrants  11, 15–21
Immortal Technique  101
informants  97, 100–102
initiation rituals  12
Integrated Ballistics Identification
    System (IBIS)  27
Internal Revenue Service  31
international crime and motorcycle
    gangs  52–53
intervention, gang  91–93
Iran  32
Iran-Contra scandal  31–32
Irish gangs  15, 89
Irish Whyos  15
Italian gangs  30, 87–89

**J**

Jackson, George  56–57
Jamaican posses  76–77
James, Frank  12
James, Jesse  12, 14, 39, 43, 83
James-Younger gang  18, 37, 84
Joe Boys. *See Chung Ching Yee*
Johnson, Jeremy  99
Jones, Kimberly "Lil' Kim"  71

**K**

Kansas City, MO  18, 38–42, 45
"Kansas City Massacre"  38–42, 45
"Keep Talkin'" campaign  101
Kellestine, Wayne  47
Kelly, George "Machine Gun"
    42–43, 84
Kelly, Katherine  42–43
Kelly, Paul. *See* Vaccarelli, Paolo
Kerr, Jim  52
Kilpatrick, Ben  39, 39, 40
King, Rodney  68
Knight, Marion "Suge"  70, 72
Korn  72
Ku Klux Klan  58, 65, 79, 81, 97,
    99, 100
Kurupt  69

**L**

Labor Party (Jamaica)  77
L.A. Bridges Program  91–93
L.A. Brims  66
Ladies of Destruction  75
*La Eme*  56, 59
*La Raza*  59
Larsen, Uffe  53
Las Vegas, NV  75
Latin American gangs  30, 59–60
Latin Kings  59, 61
law enforcement efforts and gangs
    91–102
Leavenworth Prison (Kansas)  38
Lewis, Jerry  87
Lindbergh, Charles  42
Lindbergh, Charles, Jr.  42, 45
Lindbergh Law  45
Liotta, Ray  97

liquor, ban on. *See* Prohibition era
*Little Caesar* 93
Ljunggren, Mikael 53
"lone wolf" attacks 79
Longabaugh, Harry (Sundance Kid)
    19, *39, 39*, 40
Long Beach, CA 75
Los Angeles, CA
    ethnic gangs 74, 77, 78
    ghetto gangs 65–72
    history of gangs and gang crime
      in 11
    law enforcement efforts 91–93
    Prohibition era in 27
*Los Angeles Times* 70
*Los Macheteros* 59
*Los Solidos* 59
Luciano, Charles "Lucky" 16–17,
    28, 97

## M

"Mad Dog" 12
Mafia 19, 54, 87–89, 94, 95, 96–97
Major League Baseball 95
Maricle, Robert 55
*Marielitos* 75
marijuana 28–30
Martinez, Mariano 56
Marvin, Lee 48
Marxism 57
Masters of Destruction (MOD) 75
Matranga, Charles 21
Matranga crime family 20–21
Mazzella, Dave 79
McParland, James 95–96
MC Ren 69
McVeigh, Timothy 99
medicinal liquor 25
*Menace II Society* 89
Menino, Thomas 101
Metzger, John 79
Metzger, Thomas 79
Mexican gangs 30
Mexican Mafia 58, 59, 60, 89
Miami, FL 27, 75
Mieske, Kenneth 79
Miller, Vernon 42

Missouri 18
mobs 94
MOD. *See* Masters of Destruction
Molly Maguires 95–96
Mongolian Boys 75
Mongol Nation 97
Mongols 54
Moran, George "Bugs" 12, 26
"Mother of Bandits." *See* Missouri
motorcycle gangs
    Big Four 49–52, 53
    colors 50–51
    drug markets 30
    films portraying 87
    history of 12
    international — 52–53
    law enforcement efforts 94,
      97
    one-percenters 48–49
    policing 53–54
mottos of outlaw biker gangs 51
MTV 72
Mulugeta Seraw 79
murder 13
Murder, Incorporated 97
music, gang 69, 70
Mutrux, Floyd 89
Myers, Walter 84

## N

Nash, Frank "Jelly" 38–40, 43
Nash, Jay 44
Nate Dogg 69
National Alliance 99
National Gang Threat Assessment
    66
National Institute of Health 52
National Organization for Women
    95
Nazi Low Riders (NLR) 55, 58, 61
'Ndrangheta 19
Nelson, George "Baby Face" 36, 84
neo-Nazi National Alliance 99
Neta 59–60
Newman, Paul 40, *85, 85*
New Orleans, LA 18, 20–21

newspapers, gangs and gang crime
     portrayed in  12
Newton brothers  37
New York City, NY
     "Black Hand" practice  19
     crime syndicates  28
     ethnic gangs  74, 78
     ghetto gangs  66
     history of gangs and gang crime
          in  11, 16–18
     Prohibition era in  25, 27
Nicaragua  32
Nigerian ethnic gangs  79–80
Nixon, Richard  29
NLR. *See* Nazi Low Riders
Nobel Peace Prize  67
"noble experiment"  25. *See also*
     Prohibition era
norteños  59
Northern Structure  59
North Side Gang  26
Notorious B.I.G. *See* Wallace,
     Christopher
novels, gang-oriented. *See* books,
     gangs and gang crime portrayed
     in
*Nuestra Familia*  56, 58, 59, 61

**O**
Office of National Drug Control
     Policy  29
Oklahoma City bombing  99
*omertá*  97
The Order  99
organized crime  94
Oriental Ruthless Boyz  75
Oriental Troops  75
orphans  11
Outlaws Motorcycle Club  49–50,
     51
*The Outsiders* (Hinton)  83, 89

**P**
Pacino, Al  87, 88, *88*, 89
*Paddy Whacked* (English)  89
The Pagans  52

Parker, Bonnie  37
Parker, Robert LeRoy (Butch Cas-
     sidy)  19, 39–40, *39*, 84, 85
patches of outlaw biker members
     48, 50–51
patience in law enforcement  7–8
Peckerwoods  61
Peckinpah, Sam  40
Pelican Bay prison (California)  61
Pelican Bay's Security Housing
     Unit (California)  61
Pendergast, Tom  39
People's National Party (Jamaica)
     77
Petrosino, Giuseppe  20
Philadelphia, PA  11, 18, 28, 74
Phillips, Chuck  70
*Philosophy of History* (Hegel)  30
Pierce, William Luther  99
Pinkerton Detective Agency  18,
     40, 95–96
pirates  11
Piru Street Boys  66
Pistone, Joseph  96–97
Plug Uglies  17
police
     job of  7
     law enforcement efforts
          91–102
     patience required of  7–8
Police Athletic Leagues  91, 92, *92*
Portland, OR  79
posses  76–77
prison gangs
     Aryan Brotherhood  58
     Black Guerrilla Family  56–58
     "blood in, blood out"  62
     Crips vs. Bloods  61
     *La Eme*  56
     Nazi Low Riders  61
     Neta  59–60
     *Nuestra Familia*  59
     recruitment and suppression
          62–64
     Security Threat Groups  55–56
     Texas Syndicate  60–61, *60*

probationary outlaw biker members  50
Prohibition era  23–33, 84, 94
prostitution  13
Provenzano crime family  20–21
public enemies  35–45, 84
Purple Gang  94
Puzo, Mario  87

**Q**

Queen, William  54, 97
Quiroga, Robert  52

**R**

racial holy war (RAHOWA)  81
racism  56, 58, 59, 62, 79, 81
Racketeer Influenced and Corrupt Organizations Act (RICO)  93–95, 100
RAHOWA. *See* racial holy war
Ramirez gang  77
rape  13
rap music  69–72, 89
rap wars  70–71
Rastafarian religion  77
Reagan, Ronald  29, 31–32, *31*
*Rebel Without a Cause*  87
recruitment of prison gang members  62–64
*Redemption*  67
Redford, Robert  40, 85, *85*
Red Rags  61
"Red Scare"  23
*Reefer Madness*  28
Reles, Abraham "Kid Twist"  97
Reno brothers  18
Retaliator Skinhead Nation  81
Richetti, Adam  42
RICO. *See* Racketeer Influenced and Corrupt Organizations Act
Rikers Island (New York)  61
Rio Pedras prison (Puerto Rico)  59
*Rite of Passage* (Wright)  84
Roach Guards  17
Road Knights  53
robbery  13, 37–38
rock cocaine. *See* crack

Rock Machine gang  53
Rolling Stones (band)  51
*Romeo and Juliet*  86
*Romeo + Juliet*  86
*Romiette and Julio* (Draper,)  84
Roosevelt, Franklin  28
Rowe, Gary  97
*Rumble* (Ellison)  84
*Rumble Fish* (Hinton)  83, 89
"rumbling"  12
"Rum Row"  26
Russian ethnic gangs  78
Russian Mafia  78

**S**

Saietta, Ignazio "Lupo the Wolf"  19–20
*Samahang Dugong Pinoy*  77
San Francisco, CA  27, 73
San Gabriel Killas  74
San Quentin prison (California)  56, 57, 58
Sarber, Jesse  43
*Sarzana*  78
*Satanas*  77
"Scarface." *See* Capone, Al, 89
*Scarface*  75, 89
Schrock, Daymon  55
Schwarzenegger, Arnold  59
science, role of in — solving crime  8
*Scorpions* (Myers)  84
Seattle, WA  75
Security Threat Groups (STGs)  55–56
Senate Permanent Investigation Committee  98
Shakespeare, William  86
Shakur, Tupac  70
"Shotgun Man"  19
Shower posse  77
silence, code of  97
skinhead groups  79, 80, *80*, 81, 89, 99
SLAPP cases. *See* strategic lawsuit against public participation
Snoop Dogg  69, 70, 72

Soja, Jeanne 55
*Soledad Brother* (Jackson) 57
Soledad Prison (California) 59
Southern Poverty Law Center
   (SPLC) 79
Spangler Posse 77
SPLC. *See* Southern Poverty Law
   Center
Spook Hunters 65
STGs. *See* Security Threat Groups
St. John, Billy. *See* Queen, William
"Stop Snitchin'" 102
*Strapped* 89
strategic lawsuit against public par-
   ticipation (SLAPP) cases 95
*Streets of Fire* 89
Sundance Kid. *See* Harry,
   Longabaugh
suppression of prison gang mem-
   bers 62–64
sureños 56, 59
surveillance equipment 95, 96–98,
   *96*
Sutton, Willie 37
*Switchblade Sisters* 89
Symbionese Liberation Army 58
syndicates 28–30, 94

**T**
taking care of business. *See* TCB
   Hate Crew
Tackwood, Louis 57
Tammany Hall 16, 17
tattoos, gang 50–51, 56, 59, *60*
Taylor, Jayceon "The Game" 72
TCB Hate Crew 81
Texas Bankers Association 38
Texas Syndicate 60–61, *60*
*Tex* (Hinton) 89
Thai, David 74
*That Was Then, This Is Now* (Hin-
   ton) 83, 89
Thomas, Rodney 101
Thompson, Hunter 49
*Time* magazine 87
Tiny Raskal gang 75
Tom's Town. *See* Kansas City, MO

Tone Loc 69
Tongs 73
Torrio, Johnny "The Brain" 16
train robbery 18
Tray Deee 69
Triads. *See* Tongs
*Trouble Makers* 86
Trudeau, Yves "Apache" 53
*The Turner Diaries* 99
21st Amendment 25
*A Two-Dollar Bet Means Murder*
   13

**U**
UBN. *See* United Blood Nation
*Under and Alone* (Queen) 97
undercover agents 54, 95–99
Unger, Robert 42
*The Union Station Massacre*
   (Unger) 42
United Bamboo 74
United Blood Nation (UBN) 61, 66
Unit 88 99
University of Pennsylvania 74
Urschel, Charles 42
U.S. Border Patrol 29
U.S. Coast Guard 29, 31
U.S. Customs Service 29
U.S. Justice Department 35, 66, 77
   Assets Forfeiture Fund 100
U.S. Marshals Service 99

**V**
Vaccarelli, Paolo (Paul Kelly) 16–17
Valachi, Joseph 97, 98, *98*
Vanilla Ice 70
Vargas Family 77
*VIBE* magazine 70
victimless crimes 13
Vietnam War 51, 74
Visalia, CA 75
Volstead Act 25

**W**
*Wah Ching* 73–74
Wallace, Christopher 70–71, *71*
WAR. *See* White Aryan Resistance

Warlocks  52
War on Crime  38
"war on drugs"  29, 31–32
Warren G  69
*The Warriors* (book; Yurick)  84, 89
*The Warriors* (film)  89
Washington, Raymond "Truck"
    65–66
Watts (Los Angeles, CA) riot  65
Weather Underground group  58
Wells Fargo agents  40
West Philly Woo Boys  74
Westside Connection  72
West Side Crips  65
*West Side Story*  86
White Aryan Resistance (WAR)  79,
    81
White Power Liberation Front  81
White Tigers  75
*The Wild Angels*  87
Wild Bunch  19, 39–40, *39*
*The Wild Bunch* (book; Fox)  40
*The Wild Bunch* (film)  40, 84
*Wild Hogs*  52

*The Wild One*  48, 87
Wild West gangs  18–19
Williams, Stanley "Tookie"  65,
    66–67, *67*, 68, 69
wiretaps  54
witness security  98–100
Witness Security Program (WIT-
    SEC)  98, 100
WITSEC. *See* Witness Security
    Program
Wood, John  52
World War II  51
Wright, Richard  84

**X**
Xzibit  72

**Y**
*Yakuza*  73
Yale, Frankie  16–17
*You Got Served*  72
Younger brothers  18
Yurick, Sol  84, 89

# About the Author

A former public school teacher (grades 6–8, 1979–80), Michael Newton has published 202 books since 1977, with 18 more scheduled for release from various houses through 2010. His first nonfiction book—*Monsters, Mysteries and Man* (Addison-Wesley, 1979)—was a volume for young readers on cryptozoology and UFOs. His recent reference works include *The Encyclopedia of Serial Killers* (2d edition, 2006) and seven other books from Facts on File (2000–2007), plus the *FBI Encyclopedia* and an *Encyclopedia of Cryptozoology* (McFarland, 2004 and 2005). His history of the Florida Ku Klux Klan, *The Invisible Empire* (University Press of Florida, 2001), won the Florida Historical Society's 2002 Rembert Patrick Award for Best Book on Florida History. A full list of Newton's published and forthcoming titles may be found on his Web site at http://www.michaelnewton.homestead.com.

# About the Consulting Editor

John L. French is a 31-year veteran of the Baltimore City Police Crime Laboratory. He is currently a crime laboratory supervisor. His responsibilities include responding to crime scenes, overseeing the preservation and collection of evidence, and training crime scene technicians. He has been actively involved in writing the operating procedures and technical manual for his unit and has conducted training in numerous areas of crime scene investigation. In addition to his crime scene work, Mr. French is also a published author, specializing in crime fiction. His short stories have appeared in *Alfred Hitchcock's Mystery Magazine* and numerous anthologies.